T0041870

SEED
SAVING

Also by Caleb Warnock

The Forgotten Skills of Self-Sufficiency Used by the Mormon Pioneers

*The Art of Baking with Natural Yeast: Breads, Pancakes,
Waffles, Cinnamon Rolls and Muffins*

*Backyard Winter Gardening: Vegetables Fresh and Simple, In Any Climate without
Artificial Heat or Electricity the Way It's Been Done for 2,000 Years*

Trouble's On the Menu: A Tippy Canoe Romp—With Recipes

More Forgotten Skills of Self-Sufficiency

Hand-Dipped: The Art of Creating Chocolates and Confections at Home

Forgotten Skills of Backyard Herbal Healing and Family Health

The 100 Percent Natural Foods Cookbook

Stress-Free Vegetable Gardening: Thriving Gardens with Minimal Effort

SEED SAVING

A BEGINNER'S GUIDE TO HEIRLOOM GARDENING

CALEB WARNOCK

AUTHOR OF *STRESS-FREE VEGETABLE GARDENING*
AND *BACKYARD WINTER GARDENING*

HOBBLE CREEK PRESS | AN IMPRINT OF CEDAR FORT, INC. | SPRINGVILLE, UTAH

© 2017 Caleb Warnock
All rights reserved.

The views expressed within this work are the sole responsibility of the author and do not necessarily reflect the position of Cedar Fort, Inc., or any other entity.

No part of this book may be reproduced in any form whatsoever, whether by graphic, visual, electronic, film, microfilm, tape recording, or any other means, without prior written permission of the publisher, except in the case of brief passages embodied in critical reviews and articles.

ISBN 13: 978-1-4621-1342-2

Published by Hobble Creek Press, an imprint of Cedar Fort, Inc.
2373 W. 700 S., Springville, UT 84663
Distributed by Cedar Fort, Inc., www.cedarfort.com

LIBRARY OF CONGRESS CATALOGING-IN-PUBLICATION DATA

Names: Warnock, Caleb (Caleb J.), 1973- author.
Title: Seed saving / Caleb Warnock.
Description: Springville, Utah : Hobble Creek Press, [2016] | Includes
  bibliographical references and index.
Identifiers: LCCN 2016043724 (print) | LCCN 2016046045 (ebook) | ISBN
  9781462113422 (layflat binding : alk. paper) | ISBN 9781462127580 (epub,
  pdf, mobi)
Subjects: LCSH: Seeds--Harvesting. | Vegetables--Seeds. | Fruit--Seeds. |
  Germplasm resources, Plant--Collection and preservation.
Classification: LCC SB118.32 .W37 2016 (print) | LCC SB118.32 (ebook) | DDC
  631.5/21--dc23
LC record available at https://lccn.loc.gov/2016043724

Cover and page design by M. Shaun McMurdie
Cover design © 2017 by Cedar Fort, Inc.
Edited by Jennifer Johnson

Printed in the United States of America

10 9 8 7 6 5 4 3 2 1

Printed on acid-free paper

CONTENTS

WHY CARROTS AND TOMATOES DON'T GROW AS WEEDS

The goal of all seed saving is to prevent seeds from becoming wild.

Because I own an heirloom seed company, I often get asked this question: "So if I want to save seeds from my garden, all I have to do is plant the seeds you sell and save the seeds from those plants, right?" If only Mother Nature was that simple and generous! The truth is, throughout the history of the world, people have had to work for food.

Some vegetables are easy to save seeds from. Lettuce and beans are painless. Most vegetables are not. This is because *wild pollen is always dominant*. If this were not true, weeds would be vegetables and all our lives would be much, much easier. No one would go hungry—ever. It's nice to imagine a world where patches of weeds are gardens of vegetables. But that world does not exist. (Some weeds are edible, but none of them spontaneously produce carrots, for example.) Every single heirloom food we eat was carefully selected, through natural seed saving methods, to become what it is today. (Hybrid and genetically modified plants, which existed commercially for the first time beginning in the 1920s, have been manipulated in laboratories and with unnatural pollination techniques. More on that later.)

The problem with wild seeds is that they produce unpredictable or inedible food. Let me give you examples of both.

THE PROBLEM OF UNPREDICTABLE SQUASH

Many gardeners have had "volunteer" squash appear in their gardens. This happens when a squash is left in the garden and rots. The seeds are often scattered by voles, mice, raccoons, birds, or other creatures. The next year, some of the seeds sprout. But because of wild pollination (also called wild or promiscuous crossing of pollen), the squash they produce look nothing like any of the squash you grew the year before. They have completely different—and unpredictable—sizes, shapes, colors, flavors, and growing habits. These new wild squash are called F1 in the world of genetics. If some of the seeds inside these F1 squash are left in the garden to grow the next year (or purposefully saved by the gardener), the F2 generation will also be very different from the F1 generation or the original plants. The F3 generation will continue this trend, as will the **F4** generation, and so on. If a large enough population of seeds remains from year to year, the traits of these squash will remain forever unpredictable—with one exception. Because of inbreeding, the squash are likely to get smaller and smaller over the years. This is because, in nature, the squash's only job is to produce seeds. In the wild, Mother Nature does not waste energy producing thick, delicious squash for eating if she can produce small, thin squash with viable seeds. The only way to have what science calls "true seed"—meaning seeds that will grow squash that predictably resemble the parents—is to carefully control the pollination, making sure only "like" squash can pollinate "like" squash. For example, a dark green zucchini can only pollinate other dark green zucchinis if you want the seeds to produce true dark green zucchinis. If they are pollinated by any other kind of zucchini or any other kind of squash in the same species, the results will be wild squash with unpredictable traits. They might be any color, flavor, size, and shape—and likely will be.

INEDIBLE CARROTS

In my garden, as I write this, I am growing several thousand carrots. We are self-reliant when it comes to carrots, meaning we don't ever buy them from the grocery store because we grow all we need for the year. The carrots I am growing are a mix of colors—black, orange, red, purple, yellow, and white. Every carrot is heirloom. We don't grow any hybrids or genetically modified (**GMO**) foods. Orange carrots, which are so popular today, were one of the last colors of carrots to be naturally created, through seed breeding in the 1600s by our ancestors. Natural, wild carrots are white. As hard as I try to prevent wild carrots from growing on our one-and-a-half acres, they return each year. They are noxious weeds—invasive, hardy, and vigorous. They are impossible to get rid of because they are biennial and hard to spot until they go to seed in their second year of life. And even if I could get them off our property, they grow everywhere in our state—in all fifty states, in fact.

And therein lies the problem, the eternal tension and drama that seed savers—both backyard and commercial—face every day. Carrots are one of the few vegetables in the garden whose pollen is spread both by wind and by insects, such as bees, flies, wasps, and moths. Controlling the pollen of carrot flowers *requires literally controlling the wind.*

Why control the pollen? Because wild carrots are inedible. They have a bitter, fibrous white root that is shriveled and impossible to chew, compared to the tender, sweet, healthy, and delicious roots of cultivated carrots.

Yet they are genetically the same plants.

And because they are the same plants, they easily and eagerly sexually reproduce. If the wind, or a bee, carries the pollen of a wild carrot to a domesticated carrot, literally centuries of breeding work are instantly undone. Any seeds or carrots produced from this pollination will forever be wild and unstable.

> The world desperately needs serious garden seed savers, because the knowledge of how to grow our own vegetable seeds in the backyard garden is almost lost from the world.

The world desperately needs serious garden seed savers, because the knowledge of how to grow our own vegetable seeds in the backyard garden is almost lost from the world. Very few people know how to do it successfully over years. Very few people indeed have deep experience. Yet without backyard seed savers and heirloom-only seed companies like mine, our entire seed supply will be corporate-owned and corporate-controlled for the first time in the history of the world. Read that twice.

As you begin to learn to save seeds, you will not always succeed, and this learning curve will teach you a deep appreciation of the supposedly "unlearned" generations who came before us who worked to create—and keep pure—every form of food we enjoy today. As you realize how much work went into creating modern carrots, for example, you will also become alarmed to learn how much of this food heritage is now extinct, and how few people are working to save what is left. I am one of them.

My wife often tells me that I have one of the world's worst business models. My company, SeedRenaissance.com, sells only the kind of seeds that are 100 percent natural, meaning you can save true seed from them. By the end of this book, you will know how to put me out of business, if you are willing to do the work.

HOW WILD VEGETABLES BECAME DOMESTICATED

In nature, there is only one kind of each vegetable—the wild kind. Wild vegetables are always vehicles to produce seeds. Their only goal is to reproduce. They are either roots that will produce a seed stalk (almost always in the second year) or seed pods, like cucumbers, squash, and melons, to name three.

So how did modern vegetables come to exist?

First, people learned the hard way which plants were edible and which were poisonous. Because people liked their children, this knowledge was carefully passed down.

Second, someone observed that plants produce seeds, and those seeds can be used to produce more of the same kind of plant.

Next, someone figured out that life could be better if we stay in one place and grow our own food instead of hunting and gathering. This meant the creation of the first gardens. Once gardens were created, it gave people the opportunity to really study the plants they were growing, to observe some of their natural traits. One of the first lessons they learned was this: eating everything you grow means starvation.

If you eat all the carrots, you have no carrots left to produce seed—and without seeds, the only option you have is wild carrots.

Then they learned that not all tomatoes, for example, are the same.

Tomatoes did not join popular gardening until late in the medieval age, but let's use them in this example. If you are growing tomatoes in the garden, you quickly notice a wide range of natural variation. Some are bigger than others. Some are sweeter, some tangier. Some produce earlier—a great trait if you are hungry. Some produce larger tomatoes. Some tomatoes quickly rot, but some can be put inside the house in winter to slowly ripen. People paid careful attention to all these traits, not because they were bored, but because food in the time before grocery stores was a matter of life or death. Next on the list, right below life and death, were flavor, utility, and commerce. Flavor gives life joy, and the better the tomato tasted, the more prized were the seeds of that tomato. Utility was hugely important too—the seeds of the earliest tomatoes to ripen were prized, obviously, and the seeds of the last tomato to ripen were also prized because these "long keeper" tomatoes meant the summer harvest could be extended into winter (at our house, we still use long keeper winter tomatoes, letting them slowly ripen in the dark in our garage. We pick the plants, root and all, and hang them upside down, or put the green tomatoes into egg cartons to ripen slowly).

Commerce naturally followed. Imagine this conversation, which I guarantee your ancestors had at some point:

manifested these differences unpredictably. Separating the tomatoes by traits and stabilizing the seed to make those traits appear predictably has been the work of many people over many generations.

As people became more settled, they were able to "select" more and more of these natural variations simply by keeping the seeds from the plants with the desired traits. Some kinds of tomatoes are thick and dense with few seeds,

What can I trade you for those seeds?

"What? You have a kind of tomato that ripens two weeks earlier than mine? What can I trade you for those seeds?"

Or, "What? You have a kind of tomato that slowly ripens in your house in winter instead of rotting? What can I trade you for those seeds?"

STABILIZING WILD SEEDS

Every vegetable we enjoy today has been "domesticated" by humans. I use the example of tomatoes because they are popular and most people who grow them have observed the wide varieties available. Today, you can buy certain named "varieties" of tomato, defined by their traits. We can look at the different varieties and choose the traits of the tomatoes we want to grow. But historically, wild tomatoes

and these are prized for sauces. People saved seed specifically from these kinds of tomatoes, and this trait grew stronger with each generation. Cherry tomatoes are often early and are great for snacking or salads—so seeds from those tomatoes were selected, and these traits grew stronger and more stable over time.

How did they become more stable? Well, when you save the seeds only from the best cherry tomatoes, generation after generation, you begin to weed out other traits. If our ancestors had saved the seeds from every single tomato they grew, we would just have wild tomatoes. Instead, they saw that some tomatoes were tiny, early, and delicious—and they liked them.

"Gee," they said. "I'm going to save the seeds from this cherry tomato and hope I get more like it next year."

The next year, they grew those kinds of tomatoes together, and saved the seeds from the best cherry tomatoes again, and the third year, and so on, until they had "stabilized" the cherry tomato variety simply by not keeping the seeds from tomatoes that had other traits. One of the lessons you learn in the seed garden is that it takes about ten generations of seed to stabilize a particular trait. Another lesson is grouping. If you want the vegetables to look alike from generation to generation, you have to grow those vegetables in a group. All across Europe, towns and hamlets became famous for "their" tomato or "their" cabbage. The people of those villages grew only one variety because experience had taught them that mixing plant varieties meant mixed and unpredictable results from the seeds of those plants. But if you grow one kind of tomato, the plants produce true seeds. They didn't fully understand that they were controlling sexual reproduction through inbreeding, but they did understand the results.

After ten generations (ten years) of saving seeds from the best cherry tomatoes, that "cherry-sized" trait becomes dominant, meaning the majority of the tomatoes produced by that plant will be cherry tomatoes. The more years you select for that trait, the more stable that trait becomes.

Because of this process, today we have huge tomatoes, small tomatoes, paste tomatoes, slicers, early tomatoes, late tomatoes, sweet and tangy tomatoes, winter keepers, wrinkled and smooth tomatoes, and tomatoes that are purple, black, blue, red, pink, orange, yellow, white, green, and striped. If you think I'm exaggerating, I'm not. Clackamas blueberry tomatoes are blue—and early and delicious. They are also new. They are an open-pollinated (heirloom) variety selected just recently by an heirloom seed grower in Oregon. Mother Nature provides the odd cross now and then that gives us new potential traits—but then it is up to us humans to stabilize that trait through years of work and careful selection. If we don't, the trait morphs and disappears as quickly as it appeared.

THE FIVE SEED TYPES

Recently, my wife and I took three of our grandchildren hiking on the lower Timpooneke Trail to Salamander Flat in American Fork Canyon, Utah. At the trailhead, thousands of white yarrow plants were in bloom. Because yarrow is a medicinal herb, and we grow it in our backyard for home use, our nine-year-old grandson, Xander, recognized it immediately and started examining the plants. Tens of thousands of people hike this popular trail each year, yet deep in the thicket, Zander noticed something that probably no one else had observed—a cluster of three pink yarrows among all the white blooms.

Why, he wanted to know, in a sea of white flowers does a strong pink suddenly appear?

A few people in ancient history also wondered the same sort of thing—and their rudimentary experiments to find the answer have provided us with all of the vegetables we enjoy today.

In a world filled with processed junk calories and grocery stores stocked with corporate products and startlingly few genuine foods, finding anyone who knows that carrots naturally come in a wide range of colors is rare. Finding someone who knows why one heirloom carrot is orange and another is purple and how that came to be—and what it takes to keep them that way—is almost unheard of.

Yet every single one of us is entirely dependent on these foods for our sustenance—whether we choose to eat "slow" natural foods, processed food, hybrid food, or genetically modified food (yikes). None of them exists without Mother Nature and human work.

I am writing this book so that backyard gardeners everywhere will be able to save their own true, pure garden seeds, confident in the knowledge that they can grow their own food without corporate assistance for a lifetime if they so desire.

SEED SAVING IS ALL ABOUT KNOWING FIVE THINGS

1. Which plants can sexually reproduce.

2. How they reproduce.

3. How to control reproduction to prevent the plants (seeds) from becoming wild.

4. The population size necessary to avoid inbreeding.

5. How the physical traits of genes (phenotypes) are expressed over generations (so you can prove the purity of your seeds).

Each of these five principles will be covered in its own chapter in this book. But before we get to that, let's start with this: sexual reproduction in plants is far, far more complicated than sexual reproduction in humans.

As you begin to understand this topic, it is important to remember two things:

1. You don't need a degree in botany to save backyard seeds. People have been doing this work for thousands of years. You can do it too.

2. Today, we have science to describe some of the behavior of Mother Nature when she makes seeds. But *our science is simply trying to describe and define what is happening in nature.* There are things we still don't understand—the plasticity of sexual organs among parsnips and cantaloupes, for example. In our modern age, science knows just enough to be dangerous, meaning specialists, motivated by money, know just enough to create unnatural things.

When the world began, there was one kind of seed—wild seed. Working within natural law, humans created a second kind—heirloom seed. It is critical to understand that there was nothing unnatural about these seeds. No natural laws were manipulated, and these seeds did nothing that Mother Nature was not already doing (using isolation to create an evolution of traits).

Wild and heirloom seeds were the only kind that existed until the early nineteen hundreds, when humans used brand new science to create a third kind of seed—hybrids. Hybrids are purposefully made to be unstable or sterile. In their beginning stages, all heirloom seeds were once first-generation (F1) hybrids, but growers worked for years to make them stable for the benefit of all humankind. Hybrids (unstable seeds) marked the first time in human history that vegetable seeds could not be saved by the gardener to grow more true seeds, forcing families to buy seeds every year instead of growing their own. The success of hybrid seeds was only made possible by another new invention—corporate marketing. Consumers, who initially rejected hybrid seeds, had to be convinced (some might say tricked) to give away the right to grow their own seeds, as all humans had done throughout history until this moment. Using a lie of omission ("hybrid seeds are better!") the marketing campaign has worked. What the ads didn't tell you was that there is nothing a hybrid can do that an open-pollinated (heirloom) seed can't do. The only difference between a hybrid seed and an open-pollinated (heirloom) seed is the work and years (typically a decade) required to stabilize the seed. In addition, hybrids could not exist without open-pollinated seeds. Every hybrid had open-pollinated ancestors.

Today, genetically modified seeds are created in laboratories. This is done by performing a kind of surgery, only recently possible, on the DNA of the seeds. In 2013, scientists announced they had a living sheep that glowed in the dark. The genes of the sheep embryo had been manipulated to add DNA material from jellyfish, which naturally glow in the dark. The work was complex and expensive, but the result was startling and historic—a living sheep that glows in the dark (today those scientists have a small flock). There is nothing natural about it. A sheep would never be able to mate with, and thus cross genes with, a jellyfish. But for humans, the only barrier to manipulating Mother Nature is cash. With enough money, only time will tell if there are limits—and natural consequences. With that door opened, scientists have used the same genetic splicing to create living cats, rabbits, pigs, dogs, monkeys, and fish that all glow in the dark.

Monsanto pioneered genetically manipulated seeds. They had already created the hugely popular Roundup chemical that kills whatever you spray it on, and Monsanto decided they could make huge amounts of cash if they genetically engineered corn and other vegetables so that you could spray them with Roundup and kill everything in the field—except the genetically modified corn, soybeans, and other vegetables. Today, this Roundup-ready corn is widely grown. Airplanes come in and douse the field with Roundup. Everything natural dies. The only thing that lives is the unnatural, genetically modified corn.

Only wild or heirloom (open-pollinated) seeds can be used to grow and save seeds. Some hybrid and **GMO** seeds can be saved in the backyard, but doing so is illegal and has resulted in many lawsuits.

FIVE TYPES OF SEEDS

1. **WILD SEEDS**—these seeds pollinate randomly and freely. Generally there is just one kind of each wild vegetable, which expresses the dominant genes, but occasionally recessive genes are expressed (like an albino deer being spotted in nature or pink yarrow flowers in a meadow of white yarrow).

2. **HEIRLOOM SEEDS** (also called open-pollinated seeds)—these seeds exist naturally if isolated so they don't share pollen (cross-pollinate) with any other plant in their same species. Instead of calling these open pollinated, we should refer to them as controlled natural pollination, or naturally pollinated in isolation. We should note that heirloom simply means old. In reality, new open-pollinated seeds can be made at any time. However, few are, because hybrids force you to buy seeds every year and are therefore much more profitable.

3. **HYBRID SEEDS** (antique definition)—before the technology existed to manipulate seeds in laboratories, people were able to "cross" plants (almost always within the same species only) by simply taking the pollen from one flower and putting it on another flower. This used to be called hybrid seed, meaning that pollination happened because man moved the pollen. Today, we call this kind of plant an heirloom if the seed is naturally self-sustaining through isolation when in flower.

4. **HYBRID SEEDS** (modern definition)—today, hybrids are created by methods far more advanced than simply moving pollen from one flower to another. We use science to manipulate plants and seeds. For example, all-male cucumber plants, which don't exist in nature, are created in laboratories and used in artificial pollination to create hybrids. Modern hybrid seeds do not exist in nature and cannot be created in nature.

5. **GENETICALLY MODIFIED SEEDS** (GMO)—these seeds are created in high-tech laboratories by physically removing a tiny fragment of the gene of one plant and inserting it into the DNA of another plant. When this is done successfully, it creates plants with traits found nowhere in nature. Today, plants are genetically modified to make it take longer for food to rot, so it has a longer shelf life for grocery stores. Brand new GMO apples, given federal approval in the United States in 2015, don't turn brown when they are cut.

UNDERSTANDING WHICH PLANTS SEXUALLY REPRODUCE, AND HOW

As I mentioned earlier, sexual reproduction in plants is far more complicated than sexual reproduction in humans. It might be easier to explain the basics—and then the complexities—if we start with something we can observe more easily—sex in animals. We easily understand the basics:

- A male dog and a female dog can produce offspring.

- A cat and a dog cannot.

Based on this information, we tend to think the issue is clear-cut and simple—a dog can only successfully reproduce with another dog and not with other animals. But Mother Nature is more complex. For example, a wolf and a dog can sometimes successfully produce offspring, and a coyote and a dog can sometimes successfully produce offspring.

To make things more complex, let's take a closer look at wolves. Wolves come in four species. A species is a group of animals that resemble each other and can breed among themselves but not with other species. This means that there are four kinds of wolves. They don't look alike, and they rarely breed between species. If two wolves of different species did somehow successfully mate, their offspring would be called a natural hybrid, or a wild cross. If humans used science to take the sperm of one wolf species and the eggs of another and use them to raise a wolf pup in the lab, this would be a man-made hybrid wolf. If humans used the gene from a jellyfish that allows it to glow in the dark and spliced it into a wolf's DNA to create a wolf pup that glows in the dark, that would be a GMO wolf (also sometimes called "genetically engineered" or just "engineered"). Because of the public backlash against GMO foods, the industry is trying to use new labels that don't use the words "genetically modified."

Now imagine with me that you own a purebred black Labrador dog. If you want your pedigreed dog to produce pedigreed pups, you must control the sexual reproduction of your dog by allowing it to breed with only another pedigreed black Lab. Here is what we know for sure:

- The puppies will resemble the parents.

- When sexually mature, the puppies will be able to create more purebred black labs.

Imagine for a moment that your female purebred Lab gets loose and has an amorous moment with a street dog. What kind of puppies will you have at your house? No one will be able to predict. The puppies from that union are called mutts. Here is what we know for sure:

- The puppies may look nothing like their parents.

- The puppies may look nothing like each other.

- When the puppies are sexually mature, their offspring will be unpredictable.

- If you were absolutely determined, you could possibly—with many generations of careful breeding—take one of your mutt pups and return the bloodline to a full purebred black Lab line. This would take years of work, however, and very careful breeding and selection of the offspring.

- You could take one of your mutt puppies and create a whole new breed of purebred dog from it, a new kind of purebred that had never existed before. This would take many years of careful breeding and selection.

Now, to take this example one step further, let's say it was not a stray street dog with which your dog became intimate. Let's say it was a purebred husky or collie (any breed will do). What are the results of this union? They will be almost as unpredictable as the union between your purebred and the street dog.

Wait a minute, you might say. *I might get one puppy that is mostly purebred.*

Yes, that is true. But the bloodline is still no good. Why? Because if your "mostly" purebred puppy breeds with another purebred black Lab, the results will be unpredictable. This means no one will be able to predict how much "grandchildren" will resemble the purebred mother. And the more generations you follow this breeding line, the more unpredictable the outcome will be.

Before we leave our example of dogs, stick with me for one more scenario. Imagine this: What would happen if you had a purebred black Lab and you mate your dog to one of her purebred brothers from the same litter? What happens if, year after year, in a quest for a pure line, you only allow siblings to mate? Just like humans, what happens is called inbreeding. Inbred dogs become sick, weak, and even deformed as the generations go by.

All of the dog examples we have discussed above are true of vegetables too. Except instead of having one dog to think of, you have a whole zoo of animals (a garden). In your zoo you have many breeds of dogs, all four species of wolves, coyotes, elephants, and an ark full of other creatures. And instead of only males and females, in the plant world, there are many other alternatives beyond male and female.

When saving seeds, you need to know if two plants are cats and dogs, dogs and wolves, or dogs and dogs. The answer is not usually as obvious as it is in the animal world. For example, in the vegetable world, a watermelon and a cantaloupe are like cats and dogs, but a cabbage and broccoli are like dogs and dogs. There are also rare examples of extra-species breeding, like dogs and wolves. Wild carrots and garden carrots are like dogs and wolves.

HOW DO VEGETABLES REPRODUCE?

In human sexuality, one man and one woman are necessary to produce a child. When studying sexual reproduction in plants, you have to let go of the idea that reproduction requires a male and a female.

In plant sexuality, one plant is often like a town, and one flower on that plant is like a person. One town (one plant) can provide the opportunity for many sexual unions, resulting in many children. In humans, a hermaphrodite is a person born with both male and female genitalia. In the plant world, hermaphroditism is the norm in some species. This means that one flower has both male and female parts. Unlike humans, plant hermaphrodites can sexually reproduce. Scientists call hermaphrodite flowers "perfect." Some perfect flowers—lettuce and beans, for example—have the ability to self-pollinate. Some other flowers don't.

To get started saving true seeds, it is helpful to know how seed saving has been done for thousands of years. The earliest documented seed saving is a nearly three-thousand-year-old carved stone slab from the palace of Assyrian king Ashurnasirpal II (reigned 883–859 BC) showing how pollen was gathered from the male flowers of the date palm to fertilize the female flowers.

"It had probably always been recognized, since animals were first extensively domesticated, that the fact of sex lay at the basis of whatever improvement in their characters man could bring about, for the reason that, in animals, 'breeding' has always meant the use of superior breeding animals (usually superior males) in crossing. In plants however, the fact of sex is less evident than in animals, partly because in most plants the sexes are not separated," wrote H. F. Roberts in his 1929 book, *Plant Hybridization before Mendel*.[1]

Luckily, date palms are one of the minority of plants that are either entirely male or entirely female. Because of their natural sweetness, dried dates were a cash crop three thousand years ago, as they are today. The people cultivating them quickly realized that there was not a lot of point in having male trees, which do not produce fruit. To get more space to grow more female date palms, they cut the male flowers off and shook them over the huge drooping inflorescences of female flowers, which allowed them to fertilize hundreds at a time. They may not have known the science behind what they were doing, but they knew it worked. Later, as demonstrated by the stone carving, now housed in the British Museum, they found they could just collect the pollen in baskets and sprinkle the pollen on the female flowers. Then they discovered that, just as one ram can impregnate many female sheep, one male date palm planted in a group of female palms can naturally fertilize the whole group. Today, one male is planted among 100 female palms and hand pollination is no longer done. This "grouping technology" is almost three thousand years old but is still used today to maximize the harvest by growing the fewest males possible.

This essentially remained the height of field technology for the next 2,500 years.

"It would perhaps be thought that the ancient Babylonians, having learned the art of artificial crossing in one plant, would have applied the same process to others," wrote Roberts.[2]

Before we judge our ancient ancestors for their stupidity, we can look to ourselves. Quick—how many vegetables can you name that are either entirely male or entirely female? For the past three thousand years, we've all shared one thing in common: as long as we get the food, we don't pay much attention to how Mother Nature is working out the details.

Roberts continued, "The reason for [the Babylonian] failure to do so, however, is explainable. No other economic plants with which they came into contact in their fields were similarly dioecious."[3]

"Dioecious" is a word that quickly appears when studying sexual reproduction among vegetable plants. In humans, sex is generally self-evident—a person is either male or female, or hermaphrodite, meaning a person is born with the reproductive organs of both sexes.[4] But in the world of vegetables, gender is much more complicated. Here are the basic possibilities.[5]

FLOWER TYPES

The kind of flower a vegetable plant produces has a lot to do with how seeds must be saved. In simple terms, there are a handful of basic types of sexual expression in vegetables. The science and variations of this topic go wide and deep and ultimately lead to a college degree in botany, but for the sake of backyard seed saving, we are going to discuss only the basic types and their variations.

In what science calls a perfect flower, sexual reproduction happens on the same plant in the same flower. Each perfect flower contains both male and female reproductive parts.

For reproduction to happen in monoecious plants, pollen must be moved from the male flower to the female flower either by an insect, wind, or human intervention.

"Dioecious" means a single plant is either entirely male or entirely female. These are rare in the garden, but they include spinach and asparagus. Every flower on the plant is the same sex. For best seed saving results with dioecious plants, you need double the minimum population of other kinds of vegetables to prevent genetic bottlenecking.

"Self-pollinating" means a flower can pollinate itself. However, the wind or insects can still move pollen from other flowers for pollination. To be self-pollinating, the plant must have perfect flowers. Vegetables that have perfect flowers and are self-pollinating are the "treasure" of every seed-savers garden, because these few plants produce true seeds with no

FLOWER TYPES

Pistil	the female flower organ, which contains the ovary and produces seeds
Stamen	the male flower organ, which produces pollen
Perfect flower	a flower that is bisexual (hermaphrodite) with both male and female parts
Monoecious	stamens and pistils are in separate flowers on the same plant
Dioecious	the plant is either entirely male or entirely female
Gynoecious	on one plant, all flowers are female
Andromonoecious	on one plant, some flowers are bisexual and some are entirely male
Gynomonoecious	on one plant, some flowers are bisexual and some are entirely female
Trimonoecious	the same plant has male, female, and perfect (bisexual) flowers
Self-pollinating	a flower can pollinate itself without the aid of wind or insects
Inbreeding	the plant accepts pollen from its own flowers
Outbreeding	the plant accepts pollen only from another plant

isolation needed. Peas, beans, lettuce, peppers, and most tomatoes are self-pollinating.

"Outbreeding" means the plant does not accept its own pollen and must have pollen from another plant for reproduction to be successful.

Corn is a great example of a plant that does not accept its own pollen. To complicate matters, some vegetables have perfect flowers but are outbreeding and do not accept their own pollen.

To know how a plant reproduces, you must know what kind of flower it has and whether it is self-pollinating or outbreeding. In this book, we are not going to go much deeper into this science because we don't need to. Like the ancient Babylonians, it is not necessary to have a degree in botany in order to successfully save seeds in the garden.

But, to save seeds, you must understand that in the garden, there are three possible ways for different plants to come together sexually.

TYPES OF POLLINATION

1. **WIND POLLINATION**
   The wind takes the pollen from one flower to another flower.

2. **INSECT POLLINATION**
   Insects physically take pollen from one flower to another and often take the pollen from several flowers to one flower (because pollen gets on the bee).

3. **SELF-POLLINATION**
   The plant has both male and female organs within the same flower and is able to pollinate itself without the help of wind or insects.

NOTES

1. H. F. Roberts, *Plant Hybridization before Mendel* (Princeton: Princeton University Press, 1929), 4

2. Ibid, 11.

3. Ibid, 11.

4. "How Common Is Intersex?" Intersex Society of North America, http://www.isna.org/faq/frequency

5. Courtesy of SeedRenaisance.com, all rights reserved. See the basic possibilities in the chart on page 15.

HOW TO PREVENT WILD SEEDS

THE NECESSITY AND RISK OF ISOLATION

To keep seed varieties pure and true, we must make sure that vegetables don't cross with anything outside their specific variety. For example, if the flower of a stupice tomato is fertilized by the pollen of a Clackamas blueberry tomato, the result will be unstable, unproven, feral seeds. These seeds will produce tomatoes, but no one will be able to predict the traits of these tomatoes or the traits of future generations. To guarantee a predictable result from our seeds, plants cannot be allowed to promiscuously cross-pollinate outside of their variety. Stupice tomato flowers, which are believed to be one of the few outbreeding types of tomatoes, should only be allowed access to pollen from other stupice tomato plants. This is the only way to guarantee purity.

Because of this reality, seed savers must use isolation techniques to control pollination. There are five isolation methods, but only two are widely used.

ISOLATION METHODS

METHOD 1: NATURAL SELF-ISOLATION

A handful of vegetables pollinate themselves before their flowers ever open. This method works only with peas, beans, lettuce, tomato-leaf tomato varieties, and peppers. Wheat is also self-pollinating.

Using this method means that you don't have to do anything to save seeds for the applicable plants except keep yourself from eating all the vegetables. Allow some to produce seed stalks, flowers, and then seeds. Let the seeds dry in the garden, gather them, and save them for planting in upcoming years.

There is a small chance of natural crossing using this method. Occasionally a bee might cross-pollinate a bean, for example. But this happens so rarely that it is not a big concern for most gardeners. If a natural cross does occur, you will know it because the bean seeds that you saved will not produce beans like the parents. They may differ in color, size, flavor, earliness, and other traits. This occasional natural crossing is how new beans and other self-pollinating vegetable varieties are born. If you get a natural cross and decide it is worth keeping, it will require years of selection in the garden to stabilize the traits, producing a true new bean cultivar (variety) rather than just a wild bean cross that will produce different, unpredictable traits each generation.

There is really no way a backyard gardener can get around the small risk of creating an unstable cross. Even commercial seed farms cannot prevent this risk. To seed saving enthusiasts, a rare natural cross of a self-pollinated vegetable is a chance to test the new wild seeds to see what they have to offer, and perhaps, if the seeds produce something worthy, create a new cultivar.

Before I go further in this book, I want to make a quick note about the word "cultivar." I hate it. I have been mocked by experts because in my public speeches I don't use the word "cultivar." My reasoning is simple. I detest jargon. I think it is important, as a teacher and writer, to use the words that are commonly understood by everyday backyard gardeners. I don't think it is necessary or useful for people to feel left out of a conversation or learning opportunity because the teacher uses words that people don't understand. Most gardeners don't know what a cultivar is or how it differs from a variety, nor do they care. In this book, I will use the word "variety" instead of "cultivar" unless there is a compelling reason not to do so.

METHOD 2: ISOLATION BY DISTANCE

Historically, this method was most widely used, and it is still most widely used today.

Isolation by distance means that pollen can only travel so far. Corn pollen, for example, has been documented to travel up to five miles on the wind. Commercial breeders must be able to isolate their corn from other types of corn by up to five miles in order to guarantee purity to the variety (or they must use a much more expensive and labor-intensive isolation method).

If you have two varieties of corn within a five-mile radius of each other, they could easily cross—and the closer they are, the more likely they are to cross. Once they cross, you no longer know what kind of corn the seed will produce. If you are a commercial grower like me, it is illegal to sell unstable seed, not to mention that your business would not last long—if you bought seed from a company that promised blue corn and the corn was yellow, you are not likely to buy from them again. (Yes, blue corn exists.)

Unfortunately, isolation by distance is problematic. For most gardeners it is the only choice, but it is an experimental choice. The pollen of most garden vegetables is believed to travel between one to three miles (a chart showing exact ranges is included in every vegetable chapter). Who among us can control the wind and insects surrounding our gardens for up to three miles? Most gardeners have very small properties, and we can only experiment with isolation by distance to see what happens.

Experts vary widely on the distance necessary. This is because no one really knows. The best information we have comes from experiments, educated guesses, and experience. Let me give you some examples.

If you are growing corn on naturally flat land in a windy area, the pollen might travel five miles. In a terrible windstorm, pollen might travel further. But pollen faces a fraught journey through natural barriers. If there are trees or hills between your corn and the neighbor's corn, those barriers will likely reduce the distance the pollen can travel. Buildings can help block pollen. Windless or low-wind days can help block pollen. If pollen is carried by insects, then the amount of food available to them will help determine how far those insects must travel. The population of bees in an area, for example, will also affect how far they need to travel for food. If food is scarce, the insects will travel farther, and this increases the chances that your garden will be cross-pollinated by a neighboring garden (within species).

If a bee moves pollen from your neighbor's cucumber flowers to your cucumber flowers, then the seeds produced by that cucumber will not be pure. There is no way anyone can accurately predict whether crossing will occur. We know for certain, however, that if we plant two or more varieties of watermelon, for example, in the same garden, there is almost zero chance that the insects will *not* cross pollen between those varieties. So if you want to save seeds, you must control what you can control by planting only one variety of outbreeding vegetable per year.

Cantaloupe varieties must ideally be a half-mile apart to prevent crossing, according to expert agricultural studies. But in my own garden, my Noir des Carmes cantaloupes have never crossed, even though I have no control over a half-mile radius around my garden, and my neighbors do plant cantaloupe. So far, isolation by distance of my cantaloupes has been 100 percent successful for me. But this will always be experimental growing. Just because it hasn't happened yet doesn't mean that it won't happen. I cannot control what my neighbors plant. I do not try to control the insects that pollinate my cantaloupes, because that is labor intensive and expensive, as you will see when you read about the other isolation methods.

There are THINGS YOU CAN DO to increase the likelihood of getting pure seed using the isolation by distance method.

1. Plant only one variety (cultivar) per species. This means that if you want to save radish seeds, you must only plant one type of radish.

2. Plant a large population. The more plants you have, the more likely you are to get pollen only from your garden and not from a neighbor's plants.

3. Save seeds from center plants. Bees, moths, flies, wasps, and all other pollinating insects generally start feeding at the outermost flowers (the first flowers they come to) and work their way toward the least accessible flowers, which are generally the flowers in the center of the

patch. So if you have a patch of onions going to seed, and you are worried that insects might have crossed your onions from your neighbor's onion flowers, then gather the seed you want to save only from the center of your onion patch and from the lowest flowers in the center, if possible. The more difficult the flower was to get to, the more likely it is that it was pollinated last by the closest pollen, and this makes it most likely to be pure seed.

4. **Talk to the neighbors.** If you want to save beet seeds, and you can see that your neighbor is growing something that crosses with beets, it might be worth it to knock on their door, explain that you are saving beet seeds, and offer to give them some of your seeds if they will make sure their beets, sugar beets, mangels, and chard are harvested and eaten and not allowed to go to seed.

5. **Test your seeds.** The only way to know for sure if the seeds you harvested are pure is to grow them out to see what they produce. I mentioned that my rare Noir des Carmes cantaloupes have never crossed in my garden. I know this because each year, when I plant the seeds I saved from the year before, the seeds grow to be plants that look like the plants from the year before, and most importantly, the cantaloupes on those vines look like the cantaloupes from the year before. Noir des Carmes are cantaloupes developed anciently by the Carmelite monks and nuns of France.

They look nothing like other cantaloupes. They are very dark, almost black, on the outside until they ripen, when they turn orange overnight. They have a smooth skin that is not netted. They are round but have ridges. They are very easy to tell from other cantaloupes, and if they had crossed, the cantaloupes produced by my seeds would show traits of the more traditional cantaloupes that my neighbors grow. This is an easy test.

Other varieties are not so easy to test, so you have to design a test. If you want to know if your corn is crossing, you will need to plant an unusual color of corn, like blue corn or black corn. Most of your neighbors will be planting the traditional yellow corn. If yellow kernels begin to appear in your corn (grown from your saved seeds), then you know crossing has occurred.

If you want to know if your carrots are crossing with the wild carrots that grow as weeds all over the United States, plant orange carrots and save the seeds from your carrots for three years in a row. If white carrots begin to show up by the third year, you know that crossing has happened. Keep in mind that, because genes are dominant and recessive, the cross traits will not always show up in the first generation, and the cross traits will show up little by little, instead of the whole population of carrots changing traits in one year. Because your carrots will be crossing pollen with both the orange carrots in your garden and the wild white carrots, white roots may not appear from the seeds you have been saving for two or three years.

But once the trait becomes phenotypic (this means the white color gene becomes expressed physically), it is much more likely to increase exponentially in the next generations. It is possible that if you saved carrot seeds from the **F1** generation to create an **F2** generation of seeds, and so on, for several generations, all of your carrots may become white and wild, with few orange roots showing up at all. This is how genetics works. Don't assume that because you have few, if any, white roots show up in the **F1** or **F2** generations, your seed is pure. Remember that seed saving must be sustainable in the long term. If your **F1** generation is contaminated, it doesn't matter how many generations it takes for that contamination (in this case, white roots) to manifest—it still means the seed is ruined for seed saving purposes, because it is unstable, and that instability will increasingly manifest itself in all future generations.

There are also THINGS YOU SHOULD NOT DO when using the isolation by distance method.

1. Don't assume that if you have your own beehives on your property, your garden seed is likely to be more pure. Your bees are just as likely to travel to your neighbors' gardens as your neighbors' bees are likely to travel to yours.

2. Don't assume a lot of gardeners around you are saving garden seeds. The great saving grace for backyard seed savers is that even if our neighbors are growing a garden, most gardeners just eat their produce, and they don't want to try to save seeds. It's not something most gardeners do, so that gives those of us who want to save seeds more breathing room between vegetable flowers. After all, my neighbor's broccoli is not going to cross with my broccoli if my neighbor eats all of his before it goes to flower!

3. Don't assume that seed saving by isolation of distance is impossible, no matter where you live and no matter how many gardeners near you are allowing vegetable plants to go to seed. Remember, this has been the primary method of keeping seed varieties throughout history. Start with the easy self-pollinating varieties like lettuce, and experiment with harder varieties until you know what is possible. The worst thing that can happen is that you will need to buy fresh seed stock, guaranteed pure, from me at SeedRenaissance.com. ☺

METHOD 3: ISOLATION BY TIME

This method can be tricky. Pollination only happens in the garden when the vegetable plant produces flowers. For vegetable varieties that don't pollinate themselves, the flowers must be open. Every vegetable variety takes a specific number of days to go from seed to flower in the garden. You could harvest seed from two different radish varieties in one year, for example, if you timed the planting of the radish seeds so that the two varieties would never grow up to be in flower at the same time.

For example, daikon radish roots mature to prime harvesting size in sixty days, while many radish varieties take thirty days or less. So you could plant an early radish and a daikon radish on the same day in your garden, and your early radish would very likely flower much earlier than your late radish, so the flowers of the two varieties would not be open at the same time. Because of this time separation, you could save seed from two radish varieties in your garden in the same year.

Caution: when using the isolation by time method, you have to check every day to make sure the late variety is not flowering at the same time as the early variety, or they will cross. Even a few flowers open at the same time can cross. However, this method has a lot of uses. You could plant mizuna in early spring, even in a cold frame, and allow it to flower and seed in early summer, then plant another Asian green, like pak choi, in late spring and allow it to flower and seed in late summer, as long as the two varieties never have flowers open at the same time. If the late variety tries to set flowers earlier than you want, just cut the flower stalks off before the flowers ever open. I am currently using this method in my garden to keep onion seeds pure. I am cutting off the flower heads of one kind of onion so they don't cross with another. The onions will usually try to flower again. If the first ones finish, I can allow the second variety of onion to flower. As long as the two varieties of onion are never in flower at the same time—and as long as my neighbors don't have onions in flower—both of my varieties will produce pure seeds.

METHOD 4: ISOLATION BY BAGGING

Most home garden seed savers may experiment with this for fun, but I've never met anyone who sustains this method seriously for the long term. This method is more labor intensive and is the way (along with caging) that many laboratory hybrids are created. Individual blossoms are enclosed in bags, just before the flower opens, so that no insect is allowed to enter the bloom. You can bag insect- or wind-pollinated varieties. Once the blossom opens inside the bag, remove the bag, hand pollinate the blossom, and close the bag again to keep insects out. Once the blossom dies and the vegetable begins to develop, the bag is removed. The vegetable is marked (usually with a string or tag around the vine or branch) so that it is not mistaken for a naturally pollinated fruit at harvest time. The fruit is allowed to mature as usual, and then the seeds are harvested when the fruit is mature. Sometimes the fruit must be stored to allow the seeds to mature. Keep in mind that bagging only allows you to isolate two different varieties in your own garden. Once you take the bags off, your flowers (or corn silks) are now exposed to pollination by insects or wind, whichever is applicable. If you are bagging corn, I recommend removing the bags for hand pollination only on windless days. Corn-bagging is frustrated by corn's extreme tendency toward genetic bottlenecking.

Bagging squash flowers to protect them for hand pollination is the easiest way to experiment with hand pollination methods.

I have also been frustrated with all efforts to hand pollinate carrots in my greenhouse. I grow them in winter and allow them to flower early in spring in the closed greenhouse to keep out potential wind cross-pollination, but so far I have only been able to get a few weak seeds per head.

METHOD 5: ISOLATION BY CAGING

Entire plants or groups of plants are enclosed in a cage made of material that keeps insects out. Caging only works on insect-pollinated varieties because the cage material must be fine enough to keep insects out while still allowing air and light in. If the variety is also isolated by distance from everything outside your garden, you can open the cage of one variety on one day to allow insects to pollinate the group and then open a different group a few days later, with the other cages again. This is called alternate day caging. However, if there are potential cross pollinators within the commercial minimum distance, the gardener or farmer must release new bees or other pollinators into the cage. Keep in mind the bees must be new so they won't have been in the open air to harvest pollen from neighboring land. This method is rarely used because it is expensive, labor intensive, and difficult.

PHENOTYPE EXPRESSION AND INBREEDING

HOW TRAITS CHANGE OVER GENERATIONS AND WHY IT MATTERS TO SEED SAVERS

Seed purity cannot always be defined, or "seen," in one generation of seeds.

If you allow impure pollination to occur in your garden, you will have to wait until you grow out the impure seeds to see what the damage is, meaning to see what kind of vegetables are produced. But if your first generation looks pure and wholesome, don't be fooled into thinking your lack of isolation went unnoticed by Mother Nature.

Remember, keeping seeds pure is all about managing which genes are dominant and which are recessive. "Mutt" seeds may seem pure when grown out, but any recessive genetic impurities will become more and more pronounced as you save more generations of seeds from the impure line.

When teaching a class on garden seed saving recently, I asked each person to take a moment to explain why they wanted to take the class. One woman said she had allowed some of her carrots to go to seed and had saved the seeds. She wanted to know if the seeds were any good.

"There is good and bad news," I said. "The good news is that you are taking this class. The bad news is that it can be nearly impossible for backyard gardeners to save seeds from carrots."

As you will see in the later chapters of this book, carrots and corn are the two most difficult vegetables to save pure seed from because they are wind pollinated. Corn reverts back to its wild state very quickly—often within three years (three generations of saved seeds) in the backyard garden. But carrots revert to being wild slower, which can fool many beginning seed savers, especially if they are seeking advice and guidance from people on the Internet who have little or no experience. Carrots are a classic study of the expression of recessive genetic traits among vegetables, something that scientists call phenotypes.

Wild carrots are white and grow in all fifty states as weeds. The roots, as I mentioned earlier in this book, are often shriveled, fibrous, and bitter. If wind blows the pollen of wild carrots to the flowers of the orange carrots in your garden, will the next generation of carrots be white?

The answer is found in percentages. Some may indeed be white. But remember that orange carrots have been bred to make the color orange a dominant trait. Because of this, the color of carrots produced by "mutt" (impure) seed will change slowly over several seed generations. Instead of seeing a lot of white carrots the first time you plant the original impure seeds (the **F1** generation), you are more likely to see the carrots turn white as you save seeds from the impure seeds (the **F2** generation). In generations **F3** and **F4**, the white carrots will become a larger percentage of the population. Eventually, within five to ten generations, the only thing your seeds will produce will be wild carrots with shriveled, fibrous, bitter roots.

Impurities in seeds show up faster in some vegetables than in others. In squash and corn, impurities are usually manifested in the first generation. In root vegetables, the process is often slower. Some traits are genetically dominant, some are recessive, and some are masked. This mix changes over generations. In the plant world, one generation is one sexual union cycle—two parents produce children (seeds) in one generation. When their children produce children, that is a second generation, and so on. In most root vegetables, one generation takes two years to produce. In most leafy vegetables, one generation takes one year.

Hemophilia is a genetically inherited disease where the body does not form blood clots. It is known as the "royal disease," because inbreeding in the royal family spread hemophilia through the children of Great Britain's Queen Victoria. As her children and their children were spread across Europe in arranged royal marriages, hemophilia spread with them to Spain, Russia, Prussia, and Germany. Today we make jokes about the physical problems caused by inbreeding, but in Queen Victoria's time there was no clear scientific understanding of what was causing the problem. We know, however, that marrying siblings and cousins causes something called "genetic bottlenecking." If two cousins marry, as in the case of the royals, and their children marry each other, the generations get physically sicker and weaker, with hemophilia and other problems cropping up. The reason for this sickness is, as I understand it rudimentarily, rare recessive genetic traits become more and more pronounced and dominant as the genetic pool stagnates.

The same problem can plague vegetables.

You might think, "Well, I don't need lots of seeds, so I'll just save a few lettuce seeds from one plant." Remember that lettuce plants are self-pollinating. Seeds from one flower seedpod are genetic brothers and sisters, sharing the same parents. Seeds from several pods on the same plant are first cousins. If you plant either one of those seeds, their children will be brothers and sisters (same pod) or cousins (different pods from the plant). You have now created an irreversible genetic bottleneck. No matter how many plants you save seeds from in the second and third generations, they will all be cousins of the same genetic line. All of their children for generations will be close genetic cousins. As they continue to inbreed, you will likely begin to see problems. While plants can't develop hemophilia, they can become stunted in their growth and develop abnormalities in their leaves, stalks, and flowers. If this bottleneck continues, you will begin to notice deformed plants and flowers that are sterile and do not produce seed. It is entirely possible that your entire lettuce family could become deformed and die out.

Genetic bottlenecking can be a serious problem for seed savers. Some vegetables are far more prone to it than others. Luckily, lettuce is slow to develop genetic bottlenecking. But it does happen, and it can result in smaller plants and deformed plants. Eventually, all severe genetic bottlenecks lead to sterility and the death of the seed line. Corn is quickly and severely affected by this problem, which science also calls "genetic depression" or "inbreeding." Remember that all vegetable "improvements" (modern domesticated vegetables) are not likely to be dominant, and all vegetables are prone to genetically drift back to their wild state. My experiments with corn have shown that corn will revert completely to its wild state within three to four generations. Wild corn, which still grows in South America, looks nothing like domesticated corn. Wild corn is less than two feet tall and produces a few kernels on tassels. Cobs never appear on wild corn. Within three years, the corn seed you save in the backyard can revert from eight-foot-tall, vigorous stalks with big cobs of corn to short, stunted, almost grass-like plants with a few seed kernels (and those kernels are not sweet).

Onions are also very susceptible to genetic depression, which is why you should save only onion seeds and onion seed-bulbs from the largest and most perfect onions. Anything less will result in smaller and smaller onions in your garden each year. No matter what vegetable you are saving seeds from, you should never save seeds from just one plant. If you are hand-pollinating squash, you should ideally use pollen from three different male flowers, each from a different plant. Spinach is one of the rare garden vegetables that is dioecious, meaning a spinach plant is either entirely male or entirely female. Because of this, saving spinach seeds means you must double the number of plants (twenty) that most other vegetables require (ten). Corn requires one hundred plants at the very least just for good kernel formation. (If you ever harvest corn with kernels missing on the cob, it means that silk of that kernel did not get pollinated. On corn plants, one silk produces one kernel of corn.) Corn would need at least one thousand plants for the best genetic health of seeds, and probably even more than that. This is one of the reasons that saving homegrown corn seed is frankly impossible for most backyard gardeners. You can do it, but just watch how quickly the genetic bottleneck manifests itself. The minimum population recommendations in this book are based on the various recommendations of experts and my own experience. In truth, the larger your population is, the better off you will be.

DON'T LET THE NAME
RUIN YOUR SEEDS

One of the most common questions I get is this: Do watermelons cross with cantaloupes? The answer is no. Seeds cross-pollinate within species, and watermelons and cantaloupes are different species. The real problem for home seed savers is not knowing that seemingly unrelated vegetables are actually the same species. The most obvious example of this is the plant that goes by the Latin name "*Brassica oleracea.*" This includes broccoli, cabbage, brussels sprouts, cauliflower, collards, kale, and kohlrabi. To most people, it wouldn't seem possible that broccoli and cabbage could cross. But genetically, they are the same identical plant. Only through human selection of traits has this plant been divided into two different varieties that produce different vegetables. If you let broccoli and cabbage flowers cross with each other, they will quickly revert back to their wild state, which resembles stunted collard greens. The resulting plants will still be edible, but they will never produce a head of cabbage or broccoli again.

For this reason, it is essential to know which vegetables belong to the same species. Below, I will give you a list of species by common vegetable names for your convenience. However, you need to keep a couple things in mind when you use this list.

1. LATIN NAMES CAN CHANGE

Classifying all plants on earth is an ongoing process. For most plant varieties, it is difficult to determine what species they belong to. It can take years of work and experimentation for an expert to come to a conclusion, and then the conclusion must be tested by peers, which can take more years. Conclusions and supporting data are then submitted for publication in peer-reviewed scientific journals, and finally an official classification is considered—and sometimes even voted on—by a group of scientists on the board of some official organization. All of this costs money, but because no one has coughed up the cash for the years of work this would take, to this day, we don't know all the species of the mustard and Asian greens. To make matters worse, if a Latin name is changed or if a cultivar is reclassified, knowledge and acceptance of that decision can take decades to spread. It is not uncommon to find Latin synonyms. For example, for many years tomatoes were known by the Latin name *Lycopersicon esculentum*, but then some official group somewhere decided it was necessary to change that name to *Solanum lycopersicum*. (This problem of synonyms is even more prevalent among herbs.) In addition, many Latin names have been changed in history, so if you love to read the old gardening books that are two hundred to four hundred years old and you get excited about a vegetable you are reading about, not only do you find that the modern Latin name has been changed, but also that the modern common name has been changed too. Just figuring out what the old authors are talking about can be a challenge, even though I find they often have valuable insights when it comes to organic gardening, seed saving, and self-reliance. (They had solutions to problems that modern people have forgotten entirely. For example, they know which garden plants can be used as rennet for cheesemaking, which is something that I specialize in.) To complicate matters even further, there is no "official" or government sanctioned group or deciding authority for Latin names in the United States—all of these decisions are made de facto by groups of scientists. And not everyone agrees with the changes. Seed suppliers in particular seem to chafe at what sometimes appear to be unnecessary changes to Latin names.

2. LATIN NAMES ARE MISUSED

One seed catalog might list a particular Asian green as one species, and another might list it as a different species. If you are looking to save seeds from specific varieties that are not common, I strongly suggest you get agreement from at least three sources before you trust the Latin name. A little research will show you that the same vegetable, as listed by its common name, might be listed as different Latin names by different sources. It happens all the time. Which source is right? It might require hours of research on your part before you find an answer you can trust. Pumpkins and squash are a prime example of this

problem. Pumpkins and squash come in four different common species. Knowing which is which can save you the effort of hand pollination. If you plant four varieties of the popular *pepo* species and one variety of the *maxima*, you might be able to save seeds from the *maxima* variety without hand pollination (depending on how close your neighbors' gardens are and what they have planted). But finding agreement on the Latin names of the less popular squash species (and sometimes even the popular ones) can be difficult. Most seed companies won't list the Latin names at all, for the very reasons of uncertainty that I have outlined in this list. And it is not uncommon for one source to say a squash is one species and another source to say the same squash is another species. You can try to study up on the traits of each species and make your own decision, but you quickly find that telling one squash species from another is very difficult based on phenotype (what the plants look like). Even people with botany degrees can struggle to tell the squash species apart. It does not help at all that the common names of different squash and pumpkin varieties can be frustratingly similar. For example, the white summer crookneck squash is supposedly a *pepo* species, while the white crookneck cushaw is a *mixta* species. But the seed pack or listing for both might just say "white crookneck."

3. COMMON NAMES CAN BE CONFUSING AND SHOULD NOT BE TRUSTED

Take elephant garlic, for example. This plant is not a true garlic at all. It is actually the mild bulb of a leek plant. If your elephant garlic goes to seed (and it may), it does not cross with garlic (if your garlic produces seeds) but with leeks, which can create problems for saving leek seeds. Just because it has the word "garlic" in the common name does not mean that the common name can be trusted. When you are preparing to plant a garden for seed saving, you *must always* consult the Latin name to make sure that you are not planting two varieties of the same species, which will cross and contaminate your seed without you knowing until you test the seeds the next year. Contaminated seed (wild seed) is a lot of wasted time and effort, and it is always disappointing. Consult the Latin names in this book before planting, so you know what species you have. Another example demonstrates the reverse of this problem. Many different vegetables in the garden are commonly called "beans," but there are more than ten species of beans, just to count the common ones. Just because something is called a bean does not mean that it is related to other "beans." For example, lima beans and so-called "green beans" don't cross, because they are different species.

4. IT'S POSSIBLE TO CONFUSE GROUP NAMES WITH LATIN NAMES

Many vegetable varieties within a species are divided into groups by phenotypic traits, as decided by scientists. But all of the groups within a species can still cross with each other. For example, broccoli is part of the Italica Group of the *Brassica oleracea* species, and cabbages are part of the Capitata Group of the *Brassica oleracea* species. These group subdivisions have nothing to do with sexual reproduction, and no matter what group they are in, all of the vegetables labeled as the *Brassica oleracea* species will still cross.

5. OUT-OF-SPECIES CROSSINGS ARE RARE BUT POSSIBLE

With very few exceptions, vegetables cannot successfully sexually reproduce outside their species. But there are exceptions, and to make matters worse, there are one-way exceptions. For example, artichokes cross with cardoons even though they are different species. (*Then why are they classified as different species?* you might ask. Don't shoot me. I'm just the messenger.) And chicory accepts the pollen of endive, but endive does not cross with chicory. These are an example of a one-way out-of-species exception.

A VEGETABLE SPECIES LIST

Artichokes (Globe) [*Cynara scolymus*]

Crosses only with other globe artichoke varieties. Does not cross with Chinese artichokes.

Artichokes (Chinese) [*Stachys affinis*]

Crosses only with other Chinese artichoke varieties. Does not cross with globe artichokes.

Amaranth (multiple species—all crossing possibilities have not yet been identified)

Includes *Amaranthus retroflexus*, *Amaranthus hybridus*, *Amaranthus hypochondriacus*, and *Amaranthus cruentus*. These Latin names have changed, and many outdated names are still in use. In addition, some amaranths that were once classified as one species have been switched to another. Careful research is needed.

Asian greens (Chinese mustards) [*Brassica rapa*]

Crosses with all varieties of Chinese mustards and all varieties of Chinese cabbage, broccoli rabe, and turnips. Does not cross with common mustards or common cabbage. This group covers a range of root and leafy vegetables, including Napa cabbage, won bok, bok choy, pak choi, choy sum, tai sai (tatsoi), mizuna, Chinese michihili cabbage, all varieties of turnips, broccoli rabe (but not broccoli), and more. They all cross in the garden.

Asparagus pea [*Psophocarpus tetragonolobus*]

Also called winged bean, winged pea, and Manila bean. Crosses with all varieties of asparagus pea. (Taste is not great.)

Asparagus [*Asparagus officinalis*]

Crosses with all varieties of asparagus.

Basil [*Ocimum basilicum*]

Crosses with all basil varieties.

Bean, common [*Phaseolus vulgaris*]

Crosses with all varieties of common garden bean varieties including bush, pole, snap, wax, kidney, and shelly beans. Does not cross with adzuki, fava, garbanzo, hyacinth, lentils, lima, mung, runner, tepary, or rice beans.

Beans, adzuki [*Vigna angularis*]

Crosses with all varieties of adzuki beans. Does not cross with common garden beans, fava, garbanzo, hyacinth, lentils, lima, mung, runner, tepary, or rice beans.

Beans, fava [*Vicia faba*]

Crosses with all varieties of fava beans. Does not cross with common garden beans, adzuki, garbanzo, hyacinth, lentils, lima, mung, runner, tepary, or rice beans.

Beans, garbanzo [*Cicer arietinum*]

Crosses with all varieties of garbanzo beans. Does not cross with common garden beans, adzuki, fava, hyacinth, lentils, lima, mung, runner, tepary, or rice beans.

Beans, hyacinth [*Dolichos lablab*]

Crosses with all varieties of hyacinth beans. Does not cross with common garden beans, adzuki, fava, garbanzo, lentils, lima, mung, runner, tepary, or rice beans.

Beans, lentils [*Lens culinaris*]

Crosses with all varieties of lentil beans. Does not cross with common garden beans, adzuki, fava, garbanzo, hyacinth, lima, mung, runner, tepary, or rice beans.

Beans, lima [*Phaseolus limensis*]

Crosses with all varieties of lima beans. Does not cross with common garden beans, adzuki, fava, garbanzo, hyacinth, lentil, mung, runner, tepary, or rice beans.

Beans, mung [*Vigna radiata*]

Crosses with all varieties of mung beans. Does not cross with common garden beans, adzuki, fava, garbanzo, hyacinth, lentil, lima, runner, tepary, or rice beans.

Beans, runner [*Phaseolus coccineus*]

Crosses with all varieties of runner beans. Does not cross with common garden beans, adzuki, fava, garbanzo, hyacinth, lentil, lima, rice, tepary, or mung beans.

Beans, tepary [*Phaseolus acutifolius*]

Crosses with all varieties of tepary beans. Does not cross with common garden beans, adzuki, fava, garbanzo, hyacinth, lentil, lima, rice, runner, or mung beans.

Beans, "rice" variety [*Vigna umbellata*]

Crosses with all varieties of rice beans. Does not cross with common garden beans, adzuki, fava, garbanzo, hyacinth, lentil, lima, runner, tepary, or mung beans. Does not cross with rice grain species.

Beets [*Beta vulgaris*]

Crosses with all varieties of beets, sugar beets, mangels, and chard.

Broccoli [*Brassica oleracea* Italica Group]

Crosses with all varieties of broccoli, cabbage, brussels sprouts, cauliflower, collards, kale, and kohlrabi.

Brussels sprouts [*Brassica oleracea*]

Crosses with all varieties of brussels sprouts, broccoli, cabbage, cauliflower, collards, kale, and kohlrabi.

Cabbage [*Brassica oleracea* Capitata Group]

Crosses with all varieties of cabbage, broccoli, brussels sprouts, cauliflower, collards, kale, and kohlrabi.

Cabbage [*Brassica oleracea*]

Crosses with all varieties of cabbage, broccoli, brussels sprouts, cauliflower, collards, kale, and kohlrabi.

Cantaloupe group [*Cucumis melo*]

Includes and crosses with all varieties of muskmelon, honeydew, casaba, Armenian cucumber, snake melon, Asian pickling melons, pocket melons, vine pomegranates, and vine peaches. Does not cross with watermelon. Natural abortion of 80 percent of female blossoms, despite natural or hand-pollination.

Carrot [*Daucus carota sativus*]

Crosses with all varieties of carrots and wild carrots. Wild carrots are called "White top" or "Queen Anne's Lace" and grow rampant all over the United States, making pure carrot seeds difficult for the home grower to save.

Cauliflower [*Brassica oleracea*]

Crosses with all varieties of cauliflower, broccoli, brussels sprouts, cabbage, collards, kale, and kohlrabi.

Celery [*Apium graveolens*]

Includes celeriac, which is also called celery root, and smallage, which is wild celery. Crosses with all varieties of celery and celeriac.

Chickpea [*Cicer arietinum*]

Also called garbanzo beans. Crosses with all varieties of garbanzo beans. Self-pollinating.

Chinese cabbage [*Brassica rapa*]

Crosses with all varieties of Chinese cabbage, turnips, broccoli rabe, and Chinese mustards including mizuna.

Collards [*Brassica oleracea*]

Crosses with all varieties of collards, broccoli, brussels sprouts, cauliflower, cabbage, kale, and kohlrabi.

Corn [*Zea mays*]

Includes sweet corn and popcorn. Crosses with all varieties of corn and popcorn. Annual. Outbreeding. Wind-pollinated. Extremely susceptible to inbreeding depression. Block pattern growing increases pollination. Isolate different varieties by two to five miles. Backyard seed saving is difficult.

Cowpea [*Vigna unguiculata*]

Crosses with all varieties of cowpeas. Isolation is generally not practiced.

Cucumber [*Cucumis sativus*]

Crosses with all varieties of cucumbers, including gherkins. Does not cross with West Indian gherkins, Armenian cucumbers, snake melons, or serpent gourds.

Eggplant [*Solanum melongena*]

Crosses with all varieties of eggplant. Self-pollinating. Isolate by fifty feet.

Eggplant, tomato fruited [*Solanum integrifolium*]

Does not cross with common eggplant but does cross with all varieties of Tomato fruited eggplant.

Garden peas [*Pisum sativum*]

Rarely crosses with other varieties of peas. Self-pollinating. Seed saving may be frustrated by weevils.

Garlic [*Allium sativum*]

Should not be allowed to flower for seed-saving purposes. Propagate by saving cloves. Does not cross with elephant garlic.

Ground cherries [*Physalis* species]

With one exception (tomatillos), it is unknown to science whether different *Physalis* species cross with one another. These include Chinese lanterns [*Physalis alkekengi*], Cape gooseberry [*Physalis peruviana*], wild tomatillo [*Physalis philadelphica*], strawberry tomatoes (also called Dwarf Cape gooseberry) [*Physalis pruinosa*], downy ground cherry [*Physalis pubescens*], and purple ground cherry [*Physalis subglabrata*]. Tomatillos, also called Mexican husk tomatoes [*Physalis ixocarpa*], do not cross with other *Physalis* species. All other *Physalis* species may have some percentage of crossing in the garden.

Kale [*Brassica oleracea*]

Crosses with all varieties of kale, broccoli, brussels sprouts, cauliflower, collards, cabbage, and kohlrabi.

Kohlrabi [*Brassica oleracea*]

Crosses with all varieties of kohlrabi, broccoli, brussels sprouts, cauliflower, collards, cabbage, and kale.

Leeks [*Allium ampeloprasum*]

Crosses with all leek varieties and all varieties of elephant garlic. Does not cross with onions.

Lentils [*Lens culinaris*]

Crosses with all varieties of lentils. Self-pollinating.

Lettuce [*Lactuca sativa*]

Rarely crosses with other varieties of lettuce, celtuce, and wild lettuce. No isolation needed.

Mangels [*Beta vulgaris*]

Also called fodder beets. Crosses with all varieties of mangels, beets, sugar beets, and swiss chard.

Mustard greens [*Brassica juncea*]

Includes Indian mustard and leaf mustard. Crosses with all mustard greens varieties, including Indian and leaf mustards, as well wild mustards, which grow as weeds commonly in the United States. Does not cross with Chinese mustards.

Onions [*Allium cepa*]

Crosses with all flower-producing onion and shallot varieties.

Orach [*Atriplex hortensis*]

Also called mountain spinach, French spinach, sea purslane, and saltbush. Crosses with all varieties of orach.

Parsnip [*Pastinaca sativa*]

Crosses with all varieties of parsnip. Does not cross with carrots.

Note: Juice from stems and leaves of parsnips has been known to cause skin rashes.

Peas (also called garden peas) [*Pisum sativum*]

Rarely crosses with other varieties of peas. Isolation not needed.

Peas, pigeon [*Cajanus cajun*]

Crosses only with other varieties of pigeon peas. Does not cross with garden peas.

Peppers [*Capsicum annuum*]

Includes chili peppers. Crosses with all varieties of sweet peppers and chili peppers. Does not cross with tabasco or "squash" peppers. Self-pollinating.

Note: Sweet peppers allowed to open-pollinate with hot peppers will turn hot in one or more generations.

Peppers, tabasco, "squash," and cayenne [*Capsicum frutescens*]

Crosses with all varieties of tabasco and so-called "squash" peppers. Self-pollinating.

Peppers, cayenne [both *Capsicum annuum* and *Capsicum frutescens*]

Ask your seed supplier to tell you which species your favorite cayenne seed belongs to.

Potato [*Solanum tuberosum*]

Flower-producing potatoes cross with all other flower-producing potatoes. Propagated by saving potatoes. Some potato varieties produce seeds, called TPS (true potato seed). TPS is used experimentally to create new lines of potatoes.

Radishes [*Raphanus sativus*]

Crosses with all varieties of radishes, including wild radishes, which commonly grow as weeds in the United States.

Rutabaga [*Brassica napus*]

Also called Swedes or Swede turnips. Crosses with other varieties of rutabaga, as well as all varieties of Siberian kale and Hanover salad and oilseed rape (sometimes just called rape or rapa). May also cross with fodder turnips. Rutabaga does not cross with turnips.

Soybean [*Glycine max*]

Rarely crosses with other varieties of soybeans. No isolation needed.

Spinach [*Spinacia oleracea*]

Crosses with all varieties of spinach. Does not cross with wild spinach or orach.

Squash [*Cucurbita mixta*]

Crosses with most varieties of cushaw squash, all varieties of wild Seroria squash, and silver-seeded gourds, as well as big white crookneck squash, Cochiti Pueblo squash, and others. Does not cross with golden cushaw, orange cushaw, or orange-striped cushaw. Hand pollinate.

Squash [*Cucurbita pepo*]

Crosses with all varieties of summer squash, as well as acorn, cocozelle, crookneck, scallop, zucchini, and vegetable marrow squash, and most gourds. Also crosses with Connecticut field pumpkins, delicate squash, early prolific straightneck squash, fordhook squash, scallopini squash, and Jack O' Lantern pumpkins, as well as with Howden, Japanese pie, Lakota, naked seeded, New England pie, Patisson, potimarron, Rocky Mountain pie, Rondo de Nice, straightneck, small sugar, Thelma Sanders, spaghetti (also called vegetable spaghetti), winter pie, and Xochitlan Pueblo squash, among others. Hand pollinate.

Squash [*Cucurbita maxima*]

Crosses with all banana squash, buttercup squash, Hubbard squash, turban squash, and marrow squash varieties, as well as Amish pie squash, Australian pumpkin, and others. Hand pollinate.

Squash [*Cucurbita moschata*]

Crosses with all varieties of butternut squash and cheese squash, as well as with golden, orange, and orange-striped cushaw and sweet potato squash, citrouille d'Eysines, and field pumpkins. Crosses also with Futtsu, Kikuza, Landreth, Long Island, Tennessee, Napoli, and Rampicante (also called tromboncino) squash, among others. Hand pollinate.

Sunchoke [*Helianthus tuberosus*]

Also called Jerusalem artichoke and sunroot. Does not cross. Seed is typically naturally sterile. Propagated by tuber cuttings. Perennial. Potentially invasive.

Sunflowers [*Helianthus annuus*]

Crosses with all varieties of garden sunflowers and some wild sunflowers.

Sweet potatoes [*Ipomoea batatas*]

Propagated by tuber cuttings or shoots, which are called "slips."

Swiss chard [*Beta vulgaris*]

Also called chard. Crosses with all varieties of chard, beets, sugar beets, and mangels.

Tomatoes [*Solanum lycopersicum* (or *Lycopersicon esculentum*)]

Self-pollinating and limited insect pollination. Tomatoes with stamens that extrude from the flower are believed to cross. Isolation of extruding stamen varieties is recommended. Tomato crossing is hotly debated.

Tomatillos [*Physalis ixocarpa*]

Self-pollinating. Does not cross with other *Physalis* species. Does not cross with wild tomatillos or true ground cherries. Many companies and growers mistakenly call tomatillos ground cherries, so make sure you have *ixocarpa*.

Turnips [*Brassica rapa*]

Crosses with all varieties of turnip, as well as all varieties of Chinese cabbage, broccoli raab, and Chinese mustards including mizuna.

Watermelon [*Citrullus lanatus*]

Crosses with all varieties of watermelon and citron. Does not cross with cantaloupe.

FACTS EVERY SEED SAVER SHOULD KNOW

In June 2012, a survey of children in the United Kingdom revealed that "fewer than half of 16- to 23-year-olds know that butter comes from a dairy cow."[1]

We in the United States can imagine our urban teens are not much different. But before you scoff at their inexperience, I'd be willing to wager that you, dear reader, cannot pass a test of similar knowledge about the varieties of vegetables available to you. I challenge you :). And after this quiz, I will explain to you exactly why you don't know.

QUIZ

1. Heirloom watermelons (all natural) are available in the following colors (inside the watermelon):
   a. Red
   b. Yellow
   c. White
   d. Orange
   e. All of the above

2. Heirloom carrots (all natural) are available in the following colors:
   a. Black
   b. Yellow
   c. White
   d. Orange
   e. Purple
   f. Green
   g. Red
   h. All of the above

3. Heirloom peas (all natural) are available in the following colors:
   a. Purple
   b. Blue
   c. Red
   d. Green
   e. Speckled
   f. All of the above

The answer to every question, of course, is "all of the above." This quiz could go on and on. There are far more colors and types of every vegetable available than most people ever see. Why? Because in nature, color variation happens as a natural course of life, and if you select seeds for those colors long enough, the color trait stabilizes. But several forces have combined to repress the public's access and knowledge of these available options.

First, people by and large stopped growing their own food. When I was in college in the mid-1990s I remember reading in a magazine that gardening had once again topped the list of US hobbies. In a speech recently, I asked the audience a trick question. If gardening was the nation's top hobby in the 1990s, what is it today? They guessed watching television and playing video games, and that is correct. The average American (age 15 and older) spends 9 minutes a day on "lawn and garden care" and 156 minutes a day "watching television."[2] Certainly the vast majority of that 9 minutes is lawn care, because fewer and fewer people grow gardens. Meanwhile, we know from observation that more and more people eat out (especially fast food). Fewer and fewer people seem to cook food that is not partially or wholly prepackaged.

The second reason that many people aren't aware of vegetable varieties is that food is mass-produced on an industrial scale. Growers plant only one thing—orange carrots, for example—because they are seeding huge fields with huge machines using huge amounts of bulk seed, almost always hybrid. The goal of these industrial growers is not to offer variety, but to offer bulk foods at low prices to feed the population. What we get in the grocery store is a tiny fraction of what is available, and so most people go their whole lives without ever seeing a white watermelon or a black carrot, no matter how delicious or healthy they might be (and they are!).

Lastly, as you will read in my book *The Forgotten Skills of Self-Sufficiency Used by the Mormon Pioneers*, most of the garden seed varieties available to US gardeners in catalogs in the early 1900s are now extinct for one simple reason: heirloom seeds cannot be corporate owned. Today, three huge conglomerates sell the vast majority of seeds. (At this writing, Monsanto has made a 57-billion dollar offer to buy out Syngenta. That would bring the total down to two companies.) These congomerates buy up seed companies, drop the heirloom seed varieties, and replace them with hybrids and genetically modified seeds, because those two kinds of seeds force the grower to buy new seed each year. It's good for profits, but terrible for self-reliance. I'm also convinced that having so few seeds available by so few producers—and most of them the kinds of seeds that purposefully don't produce new true seeds—is a national security issue. Our food supply is at risk.

Most people are too busy watching television to care.

Gardening—working to provide your own food with great flavor and nutrition—is out of favor. Seed saving, because it requires extra work, attention, and space in the garden, has only been practiced among a small percentage of gardeners for the past century anyway, so you can imagine that today, the art is nearly extinct. People with a broad working knowledge of how to save seeds in a backyard garden are few and far between.

There is some information on the Internet about saving seeds. The vast majority of it is woefully inadequate because it is what I call "telephone game" information, by which I mean it is information that someone got from someone, who got it from someone else, who got it from another website, which got it from another website, and on and on. There is very little firsthand experience represented. I want you to know that this book is the culmination of years of my hard-won experience, and this book is the book I wish I had been able to find when I first started growing my own vegetable seeds, long before I became the owner of a vegetable seed company and the creator of new open-pollinated (heirloom) vegetable varieties.

Seed saving is both necessary and in crisis. We, today, are the first generations on earth who has entirely walked away from the concept of growing our own food. Through the history of the world, people grew their food—and saved their own pure seeds. Today's world is the mirror reverse—we buy our food without ever knowing who grew it or where it came from. And most of the US population today has no earthly idea how to grow and harvest pure seeds from the garden.

Even a century ago, this would have been unfathomable.

As a nation, we have spent little time making sure our children know how to grow even the easiest of vegetables. Knowing how to feed a family or a community self-reliantly is laughable—after all, we have grocery stores and the industrial agricultural complex to take care of our needs, right? They will never let us down. Our food system will never be in doubt.

Right?

I'm not fearmongering. The point I want to make is that the "zombie apocalypse" has descended on our nation twice before. Both times it nearly cost us everything. I have a large collection of ration books, stamps, tokens, and guidebooks from both World War I and World War II. I have vegetable ration stamps, sugar stamps, and stamps for tires and gasoline. I have the ration stamps that were carried by families both in the United States and working in the European theater of war. I give a lot of speeches, and I take this collection with me to nearly every speech, because most people have never seen these relics of our near national starvation. I promise you that when my great-grandparents were children around 1900, no one thought national starvation was on the horizon. Yet without war victory gardens, starvation is what would have happened. Twenty years later, we found ourselves facing starvation again. With so many of our men at the battle front, we had exactly enough domestic food production to either feed the people of the nation or feed the millions of soldiers we sent overseas—but not both. Again, it was victory gardens to the rescue. Without them, we would have lost the war. As it turns out, when you arrive to fight Nazi Germany, you can't knock on their front door and then ask for their nearest grocery store.

But that is all ancient history, and surely we will never again need to be self-reliant. Surely.

I pray it is so.

You can discern where this is going. Let's all say it together now: "Those who fail to remember history are doomed to repeat it."

Every single day, this history of abandoning self-reliance is being repeated somewhere in the world.

Today, as I write this, it is Tuesday, July 14, 2015. Half a world away from me, in Greece (where I have spent some time), people of all ages have spent their entire day waiting in lines at ATMs, hoping to get about sixty dollars out of their account. The Greek banking system has collapsed. Why? Two reasons. First, the Greeks have not been self-reliant for many years. They made a national habit of spending more than they earn, while borrowing to make up for the shortfall. Now they have failed to make the basic payments on those loans. Their lenders have (rightfully) refused to lend more money, which has caused the collapse of their economy. Second, they have a national habit of tax evasion—refusing to pay an honest tax. They want someone to pave their roads, but they don't want to pay for it.

Within hours, as I write this, the world will find out if the Greek parliament will accept what is probably the most punishing national loan agreement in modern history. If the Greeks refuse their creditors' terms, they will be forced to begin printing a new national currency. Every penny that anyone has in Greek banks will suddenly be worthless. The banks in Greece have been shut down for two weeks. Global media is reporting that what the Greek people need most desperately is food and medicine. Are you shocked to learn that they import most of both—and now, with their banking system collapsed, they can get neither? The rest of Europe has begun putting together a humanitarian aid effort for the Greek nation, the birthplace of democracy.

History repeats.

It's not just Greece. I could be telling you a similar story about what is happening on this very day in the Ukraine, Syria, Haiti, Puerto Rico, Afghanistan, and in hundreds of other pockets of desperation and war around the world.

The Greek problem is 6,300 miles away from my garden and me. Yet there is a broad sense of unease even in the idyllic small town where I live. Dozens of my otherwise normal neighbors have been participating in cottage meetings for months, drawing up plans to hightail it to the local mountains because of a growing rumor of what amounts to another national "zombie apocalypse." They have been buying powdered dried foods in bulk, along with camping and survival gear. (When they asked my wife and me to join their cottage meetings, I laughed so long and hard that they got offended and have not brought up the subject again. Why anyone would want to spend winter in the mountains in a tent with their children—or think that is a good idea, even in the "zombie apocalypse"—is beyond me. Think, people, think!)

It is not just preppers-gone-wild either. A couple of years ago, when a series of small earthquakes destroyed a few homes in a town two hours west of where I live, suddenly the local grocery stores were cleaned out. Rice, beans, wheat—any dried food item that could be stored suddenly vanished, all because of rumors that these earthquakes might just portend something larger.

When it comes down to it, we are all surrounded by wars, rumors of wars, famine, and bloodshed. We just hope that these things will stay away from us. Deep down, though, we fear we are not prepared to take care of ourselves, whether it be an earthquake, a tornado, or domestic terrorism of the power grid or water supply that descends upon us.

Remember what happened in New Orleans after Hurricane Katrina? Eventually, everyone was rescued. Well, mostly everyone—1,833 people died, and tens of thousands more suffered hunger, thirst, and the lack of clean drinking water and basic sanitation and medical care while waiting for the "government" (us, the people of the nation) to come to their rescue. One lesson we learn over and over again in a crisis is that the local government and hospitals are the first to be overwhelmed.

THINGS TO REMEMBER

Seeds only exist if someone grows them, year after year after year.

- Only open-pollinated (heirloom) seeds can be used for seed saving.

- Hybrid and genetically modified seeds cannot be used to sustainably or legally save seeds.

- Hybrid seeds are unstable or sterile (example: seedless watermelons).

- Genetically modified seeds are corporate-owned, and the US Supreme Court has ruled that all **GMO** seeds belong to their creator, even if pollination was unintentional. This means you can be sued for saving and replanting seeds that have been wind-pollinated with genetically modified pollen owned by Monsanto and other corporations. Monsanto has filed and won thousands of such court cases.

- All hybrid seeds have heirloom parents or grandparents somewhere in their family tree.

- The only difference between a hybrid seed and an open-pollinated seed is stabilization. Many companies perpetuate a half-truth about hybrid seeds, saying that they are "better" than natural seeds because they are more disease resistant or produce an improved vegetable. What they don't tell you is that heirloom seeds do the same things, except they have been stabilized over generations to make those traits permanent, and the seeds become available to anyone who knows how to grow them. *Any hybrid seed could be stabilized to become open-pollinated.* The only things that stop that from happening are first, the years (plant generations) required, and second, legal ownership. I could stabilize any hybrid seed on the market if I was willing to put in the years of work required (at least ten to stabilize a trait). But if I did, I could be sued for stealing someone's patented seed. There are special laws in the United States that provide patent protection for plant varieties, making it illegal for anyone but the creator to sell the rights to those seeds. Eventually, those patents expire, but the parentage and artificial pollination techniques used to create the seeds remain secret, proprietary information—and without that information, it may be impossible to stabilize the seeds. I will also note that if a hybrid seed cannot be stabilized, it should, in my humble opinion, be classified as genetically modified and not hybrid. The problem with cutting-edge hybridization techniques is that they begin to blur the lines between what is hybrid and what is genetically modified—and because of consumer backlash against genetically modified seeds, none of the big producers are willing to reveal or even discuss how hybridization has begun to resemble genetic modification.

- Today, in most cases, hybrid seeds are the product of multi-generation hybrids and plants that have been artificially and unnaturally bred to be all male or all female.

- Genetically modified seeds can only be created in a laboratory. They are the legal property of their corporate parents.

If you want to know the details of how hybrids are created, there is a textbook called *Hybrid Cultivar Development* edited by S. S. Banga and S. K. Banga, now out of print.

Be prepared to learn—just as a beginning example—the differences between "heterosis," "heterozygosis," "inbreeding depression," "outbreeding depression," "gametes," and "alleles." And then ask yourself—wouldn't the security of our food supply be much better off if almost all the seeds sold today were *not* so artificially produced? What would happen if, heaven forbid, some kind of crisis or contamination meant these industrialized, highly modified, -owned seeds were not available? How long would it take us, as a nation, to produce a large enough supply of heirloom seeds to feed ourselves—and how many millions would starve while we struggled to grow out the seeds necessary to feed the nation if industrial hybrid seeds were not available?

NOTES

1. Rob Preece, "One in Ten Young Adults Think Eggs Come from Wheat as Survey Reveals Our Shocking Lack of Food Knowledge," *The Daily Mail*, June 14, 2012, http://www.dailymail.co.uk/news/article-2159174/LEAF-survey-One-young-adults-think-eggs-come-wheat.html.

2. U.S. Bureau of Labor Statistics, "American Time Use Survey—2014 Results," June 24, 2015, 10 (Table 2), http://www.bls.gov/news.release/archives/atus_06242015.pdf. The average American (age 15 and older) spends 9 minutes a day (0.15 of an hour) on "lawn and garden care" and 156 minutes "watching television" (2.60 hours).

QUESTIONS ABOUT THIS BOOK

Question: Is it the end of the world if I save seeds from cross-pollinated flowers? Isn't everyone taking this a little too seriously?

Answer: It is not the end of the world, as long as the commercial heirloom varieties remain available to purchase. But each year, more of them are being allowed to die out because seed companies are being purchased by the hybrid and genetically modified seed suppliers who see little profit in heirlooms, which cannot be corporate owned. And Mother Nature has her own punishments for allowing seeds to cross. If you save seeds from crossed squash, for example, they are immediately "untrue," meaning what you get from those seeds will be wildly unpredictable. If you save seeds from a zucchini that was allowed to cross with something else, you are likely to get anything but a zucchini. But if you let several varieties of green celery cross, you might just have created your own home breed of celery, which you might enjoy for many years to come. Some vegetables tolerate crossing more than others. Corn, carrots, and squash quickly begin reverting to their wild state if crossed. Other vegetables revert more slowly. If you allow several varieties of cantaloupe to cross, the results will be unpredictable, but they might also be fine eating—so you might not care. However, most gardeners want to know what they are going to get when they plant a seed in their garden. Seeds with unpredictable outcomes are not generally beloved.

Question: Why is there disagreement among expert sources about the minimum number of plants needed to avoid genetic bottlenecking in backyard seed saving?

Answer: When it comes down to it, any answer to this question is arbitrary. What modern science knows is that genetic bottlenecking (weak plants) occurs when there is not enough genetic mixing among plants. Some vegetables are more susceptible to genetic bottlenecking than others. Corn, for example, is extremely affected when too few plants are mixing pollen. This is because modern corn has almost no resemblance to its natural self, meaning the plants in our garden look nothing like corn plants still found in the wild in South America. Humankind has bred these plants to be what we want them to be, making big ears of corn that don't occur in nature. Corn is also outbreeding, meaning that it must have pollen from other plants. Other plants, such as wheat, are inbreeding, meaning they pollinate themselves. Inbreeding vegetables are much less susceptible to genetic bottlenecking, but still appear to do best when planted in groups. Some seed growers may say you need twenty-five plants minimum to save seeds from lettuce, for example, but I say ten plants will do.

The science part of all of this is evolving. Instead of trying to give specific numbers, some experts have begun offering this advice: If the seed stock was historically limited, it should remain limited. If it was large, it should remain large. For backyard seed savers, the number of plants will likely always need to be limited because of space. We also know that, through the centuries, most seeds were saved from gardens with a small number of plants—dozens to hundreds—and certainly not thousands. The final answer comes down to what a backyard garden (1) needs, and (2) can provide. Do you need the seeds from twenty-five lettuce plants—which would produce tens of thousands of seeds? And do you have space to allow twenty-five plants to bolt to seed? If you do, then you can use a larger number of plants. If you don't, then plant the minimum number of plants instead.

Question: Why did you omit the sub-group, or sub-species, names from various vegetable varieties?

Answer: To avoid confusion. For example, within the *Brassica oleracea* species, there are a handful of vegetable subgroups used by taxonomists to help define the characteristics of similar plants. Brussels sprouts are correctly labeled as "*Brassica oleracea* Gemmifera Group," while kale and collards are correctly labeled as "*Brassica oleracea* Acephala Group," and cabbages belong to the Capitata Group. But all sub-groups of *Brassica oleracea* are sexually compatible and will easily cross-pollinate with each other. I avoided listing the group names for fear that people would be confused into thinking that the "*Brassica oleracea* Gemmifera Group," for example, is sexually different from (does not cross with) "*Brassica oleracea* Acephala Group." They do cross.

Question: Why did you repeat the same information several times in the book, for example, giving the same seed collecting instructions for several varieties of *Brassica*?

Answer: To make this book an instant reference. My problem with the various seed-saving books available on the market is that they are sometimes difficult to use. As busy gardeners, you and I should not be expected to memorize whether leeks cross with onions (they don't) or whether collard seeds shatter or not. It was important to me to have everything I need to know in each chapter. I don't want to have to read about cabbage seeds in one chapter, then flip to another chapter for instructions on harvesting cabbage seed, then flip to another chapter for an explanation of technical versus practical isolation distances for cabbages. So even though the information is repeated, you will be able to grab this book, flip to the chapter on broccoli, for example, and have all the information you need in one place.

Question: Suzanne Ashworth already wrote the "Bible of seed saving." Does the world need your book?

Answer: Yes, desperately. Frankly, I am going to tread very carefully as I answer this question, both because Suzanne Ashworth has a legion of followers and because I love her book and absolutely rely on it. But her book and this book are different like night and day.

Suzanne Ashworth has been a godsend for tens of thousands of gardeners who are attempting to learn to save seed. Her book, titled *Seed by Seed*, finally put a whole bunch of credible technical information into one place. I rely on her book for my technical work. But while the book is thorough, credible, technical, and an absolute necessity for people hoping to save the rarest heirlooms from extinction, it is not always easy to interpret if you are a backyard gardener. Ms. Ashworth—with whom I have traded seeds several times—is focused on absolute purity and technical ability. With all due respect, her book lacks critical information for backyard seed savers—regular families who are trying to save seed to save money or for fun.

For example, *Seed to Seed* will tell you that you must cage certain vegetable types, and add bees to the cage, in order to save seed. And this is true if you are working with the rarest seed in the world. But no backyard gardener is likely to spend the time and money such a method requires—especially if it is not necessary. And most of the time, such strict measures are not needed. How do we know this is true? Because caging vegetables and adding bees is not the way seed has been saved throughout history. These same seeds that we enjoy today were always saved by the historic equivalent of backyard gardeners, without any special equipment. Such modern technical requirements can intimidate gardeners from even attempting to save seed, and that is not the goal of the seed saving movement. You could get the impression from Ms. Ashworth's book that you would need many acres of land to save vegetable seeds. If that were true, very few of us in the world today could successfully save pure seed. So again, while Ms. Ashworth's book is critical for technical precision when handling rare seeds, it is not focused on being a practical guide for backyard growers of seed for home use.

Question: Are all organic seeds heirloom?

Answer: No. Being labeled and sold as "organic" has nothing to do with being open-pollinated. Organic simply describes the conditions used to grow the plants that produced the seeds. Hybrid and genetically modified seeds can be organic too, and some are sold as organic.

Question: In each vegetable chapter, you start with a quick-reference list of facts about that plant. Can you define the terms you outline?

Species:	This is the Latin name of a plant's biological classification. You must know a vegetable's species, by Latin name, in order to know what other plants and plant varieties (cultivars) it is sexually compatible with.
Easy to save seeds?	This refers to whether it is easy or difficult for backyard gardeners to save seeds from the vegetable in question.
Varieties available:	This tells you how many kinds of this particular vegetable there are. This is important, because for most vegetables, having two kinds in the same garden at the same time ruins your chance of saving true seed.
Lifespan of plant:	Plants are categorized as annuals, biennials, or perennials, depending on their lifespan. This has a direct impact on when they produce seeds.
Lifespan of seed:	Knowing how long seeds will last in storage tells you how often you have to grow certain varieties.
Seed maturation:	This describes when to gather the seeds. Gathering seeds too early or too late can ruin some seed crops.
Flower type:	The kind of flower a vegetable produces has a direct impact on how the plant must be isolated for seed purity.
Sex type:	Some vegetables accept pollen from the same plant, and some don't.
Crosses with:	A list of the vegetables that cross with each other, by common name, and any possible interspecies crosses.
Pollination type:	There are three types of pollination.
Seeds in what year?	Plants called "annuals" produce seeds and then die within one year. Other vegetables don't produce seeds until the second year of life, and then they die. Others will begin producing seeds in the second year and continue producing for many years.
Isolation distance:	The commercial minimum distances required for seed purity.
Shattering rate:	How quickly the seeds may fall to the earth and be lost in the garden if not gathered soon enough.
Population minimum:	The minimum number of plants required to avoid inbreeding.
Seed cleaning method:	How to separate seeds from the chaff.

ASIAN GREENS (CHINESE MUSTARDS)

SPECIES:	*Brassica rapa*
EASY TO SAVE SEEDS?	Likely yes, if planting one variety per year within one species. Note: Birds will compete with you for the seeds.
SEED TYPE REQUIRED FOR SEED SAVING:	Heirloom (open-pollinated) seeds (available at *SeedRenaissance.com*).
NUMBER OF VARIETIES AVAILABLE:	At least dozens in the US. This species covers a range of root and leafy vegetables, including napa cabbage, won bok, bok choy, pak choi, choy sum, tai sai (tatsoi), mizuna, Chinese Michihili cabbage, all varieties of turnips, broccoli raab (but not broccoli), and more. They all cross in the garden.
LIFE SPAN OF PLANT:	Biennial or annual, depending on the cultivar. Annuals can be biennial when protected in winter.
LIFE SPAN OF SEED:	Germination decreases after five years of ideal storage. Ideal storage means avoiding drastic temperature fluctuations by keeping seeds in a cool, dark, dry place.
SEED MATURATION:	Allow seeds to fully dry in the garden before harvesting.
FLOWER TYPE:	Perfect
SEX TYPE:	Outbreeding
CROSSES WITH:	All varieties of Chinese mustards and all varieties of Chinese cabbage, broccoli raab, and turnips. Does not cross with common mustards.
POLLINATION TYPE:	Insect-pollinated
SEEDS IN WHAT YEAR?	Annuals within this species produce seeds in the first year. Biennials produce seeds in the second year.
ISOLATION DISTANCE:	Isolate different varieties by one mile.
SHATTERING RATE:	Quick
POPULATION MINIMUM:	10+ plants

SEED-CLEANING METHOD

Thresh and winnow. When the seedpods are dry, rub them to release the seeds, or uproot the plant carefully and hit it against the inside of a large box or plastic storage container to release and capture the seeds. Be careful when touching the dried plant in the garden, because the slightest shaking can cause hundreds of seeds to fall to the ground. You may want to place an old sheet on the ground under the plant before trying to harvest seeds or uproot the plant.

RECOMMENDED VARIETIES

Chinese Michihili Cabbage

Excellent fall and winter greens. Grows outdoors for fall and in a greenhouse or cold frame for winter. In winter, this cabbage is not likely to form a full head. Harvest the leaves for salads and Asian-inspired dishes. Available at SeedRenaissance.com.

Mizuna

Winner! This Asian green is a winter wonder—it pops up in my geothermal greenhouse despite the cold nights. It grows very fast—even in January—faster and more reliably than other winter greens; it grows prolifically. Cut at ground level and it will grow back over and over. And it's just fun to look at with its bright green frisée leaves. Mizuna is great for salads. Available at SeedRenaissance.com.

Purple Top Globe Turnip

This has a wonderful heirloom turnip taste, and it's a very hardy plant that's great for using in roast vegetable dishes and soups. It has a beautiful purple ring around a white globe with white flesh inside. It's an excellent self-seeder as long as you keep it isolated from other turnips and broccoli raab. Available at SeedRenaissance.com.

Komatsuna

This Japanese vegetable grows very fast in cold soil, making it ideal for winter cold frames, hot beds, and greenhouses. This is about a week slower than mizuna and has a nice flavor. Cut at ground level and it will grow back over and over. It's bright green and great for salads. Available at SeedRenaissance.com.

Sacrificial Tai Sai (for salad greens or organic pest control)

Winner! This Asian green works better than any other in my trials of sacrificial plants. It's one of the best organic methods for dealing with slugs and aphids—simply let them flock to this plant, which they love, and they will leave your other plants alone. Works like magic, especially in greenhouses, cold frames, and hot beds—and in the open garden. Available at SeedRenaissance.com.

HOW TO SAVE SEEDS

Let at least ten plants of the same variety go into flower. It is possible that insects may cross-pollinate your plants with your neighbor's plants if your neighbor is growing any kind of *Brassica rapa* varieties, including turnips, and they are in flower at the same time as yours. As the seedpods form, the plant will naturally begin to die back and dry up.

The seedpods of all Asian greens plants will shatter to naturally disperse the seed, usually beginning with the topmost seedpod. There are two methods for collecting the seed before the pods shatter so that it is not lost. The first method, which I do not recommend, is to check the plant each evening and gather the pods that have begun to crack. This will take about three weeks. This method is laborious. The second method is best. As soon as the first seedpod cracks, pull up the plants by the roots, put them upside down into a paper bag or pillowcase, and allow them to air dry in shade, not in direct sunlight. The nutrients contained in the roots and stem will give the remaining seed enough food and time to mature. When using this method, perhaps 20 percent of the seed will not have time to fully mature and therefore will never germinate, but I think it is far better to sacrifice the fertility of one-fifth of the seeds in order to save the time it would take to gather pods each day over a period of three weeks using the first method. When the bagged plants are fully dry, you should wear leather gloves and strip the seedpods from the dried plants. The dried plants should still be in the bag while you do this so that the seed is collected in the bag as you work. The chaff (crushed pods and dried leaves) is then separated from the seed by pouring the seed onto a sheet of cloth or plastic during a wind. The seeds will drop to the sheet and the chaff will blow away. You will likely need to repeat this chaffing method several times. Seed does not need to be perfectly clean for home use.

Pak choi

ASPARAGUS

SPECIES:	*Asparagus officinalis*
EASY TO SAVE SEEDS?	No
SEED TYPE REQUIRED FOR SEED SAVING:	Heirloom (open-pollinated) seeds (available at SeedRenaissance.com).
NUMBER OF VARIETIES AVAILABLE:	Several
LIFE SPAN OF PLANT:	Perennial
LIFE SPAN OF SEED:	Germination decreases after five years of ideal storage. Ideal storage means avoiding drastic temperature fluctuations by keeping seeds in a cool, dark, dry place.
SEED MATURATION:	Pick seed berries in late fall, age indoors for several weeks until wrinkled, and scrape out berries. Dry the seeds before storing them.
FLOWER TYPE:	Dioecious
SEX TYPE:	Outbreeding
CROSSES WITH:	All varieties of asparagus
POLLINATION TYPE:	Insect-pollinated
SEEDS IN WHAT YEAR?	The second year and onward
ISOLATION DISTANCE:	Isolate different varieties by two miles.
SHATTERING RATE:	Does not shatter
POPULATION MINIMUM:	20+ plants

Asparagus (male)

SEED-CLEANING METHOD

Scrape seeds from within berries when mature. Dry seeds before storage.

Note: Hybrid species have been manipulated to produce only male spears without female spears.

RECOMMENDED VARIETIES

Mary Washington Asparagus

Known for its long, thick spears, productivity, and flavor, this asparagus has the ability to hold its flavor when frozen—if you can stop yourself from eating it immediately. This variety is a favorite for flavor. Available at SeedRenaissance.com.

HOW TO SAVE SEEDS

True seeds can be saved only from heirloom varieties. In autumn, the female plants will produce red berries. Pick these seed berries in late fall and then age them indoors for several weeks until they begin to wrinkle. Scrape the seeds from the berries and dry the seeds before storage. Another method is to divide the root clumps in half in autumn and transplant one half to a new location.

Asparagus (female)

BASIL

SEED-CLEANING METHOD

Thresh and winnow. Sweet basil is probably the most popular culinary herb in the US, with good reason. The flavor and aroma of fresh basil are beyond compare.

RECOMMENDED VARIETIES

Sweet Basil (Ocimum basilicum)

This is the herb we use the most at our house—on pasta and roast. Can you even make tomato pasta sauce without fresh garden basil? Available at SeedRenaissance.com.

Cinnamon Basil (Ocimum basilicum)

A basil plant with a cinnamon flavor. Fun to grow, and easy to use in any dish where you want a cinnamon flavor. May be used dried or fresh. Plant directly in the garden after all danger of frost has passed, or indoors up to four weeks before your last frost date. Available at SeedRenaissance .com.

Lime Basil (Ocimum americanum)

This is a basil plant with a wonderful lime flavor! It's fun to grow and easy to use in any dish where you want a lime flavor. It may be used dried or fresh. Plant directly in the garden after all danger of frost has passed, or plant indoors up to four weeks before your last frost date. Please note, this variety does not cross with sweet basil or cinnamon basil. Available at SeedRenaissance.com.

SPECIES:	Ocimum basilicum
EASY TO SAVE SEEDS?	Likely yes, if planting one variety per year within one species.
NUMBER OF VARIETIES AVAILABLE:	Sweet basil, lime basil, lemon basil, cinnamon basil, chocolate basil, holy basil, miniature basil, and others. Some varieties are different species.
LIFE SPAN OF PLANT:	Annual
LIFE SPAN OF SEED:	Germination decreases after five years of ideal storage. Ideal storage means avoiding drastic temperature fluctuations by keeping seeds in a cool, dark, dry place.
SEED MATURATION:	Allow seeds to dry fully on the plant in the garden.
FLOWER TYPE:	Perfect
SEX TYPE:	Inbreeding
CROSSES WITH:	All varieties within the same species
POLLINATION TYPE:	Insect-pollinated
SEEDS IN WHAT YEAR?	First year
ISOLATION DISTANCE:	Disputed. Expert opinions range from 150 feet to ½ mile between varieties.
SHATTERING RATE:	Slow
POPULATION MINIMUM:	10+ plants

HOW TO SAVE SEEDS

Allow at least ten plants to go to flower and produce seed. The spikes of flowers will begin to lose their petals, usually beginning at the bottom, with new flowers blooming at the top of the spike. Allow the spike to begin to dry, and pull up the whole plant by the root. Knock the soil from the roots. Put the plant in a paper bag or cloth pillowcase to air-dry out of direct sunlight for several days. When the plant is fully dry, shake the bag or pillowcase vigorously to dislodge the seed, or using leather gloves, strip the dried seedpods, letting them fall into the bag or pillowcase. Then rub the pods together.

Note: Basil seedpods are unusual to find in the garden because they are never closed. The pods are always open to the air at the bottom, and the basil seed will fall out of the pods in a wind if the plants are allowed to fully dry in the garden.

BEANS

SPECIES:	Common bean [*Phaseolus vulgaris*] crosses with all common garden bean varieties including bush, pole, snap, wax, kidney, and shelly beans. It does not cross with other bean species listed in this chapter.
	Adzuki bean [*Vigna angularis*] crosses with all varieties of adzuki beans. It does not not cross with other bean species listed in this chapter.
	Fava bean [*Vicia faba*] crosses with all varieties of fava beans. It does not cross with other bean species listed in this chapter.
	Garbanzo bean [*Cicer arietinum*] crosses with all varieties of garbanzo beans, which are also called chickpeas. Garbanzo beans do not cross with other bean species listed in this chapter.
	Hyacinth bean [*Dolichos lablab*] crosses with all varieties of hyacinth beans. It does not cross with other bean species listed in this chapter.
	Lentils [*Lens culinaris*] cross with all varieties of lentil beans, but do not cross with other bean species listed in this chapter.
	Lima bean [*Phaseolus limensis*] crosses with all varieties of lima beans, but does not cross with other bean species listed in this chapter.
	Mung bean [*Vigna radiata*] crosses with all varieties of garden mung beans, but does not cross with other bean species listed in this chapter.
	Rice beans [*Vigna umbellata*] crosses with all varieties of rice beans, but does not cross with other bean species listed in this chapter.
	Runner bean [*Phaseolus coccineus*] crosses with all varieties of runner beans, but does not cross with other bean species listed in this chapter.
	Tepary bean [*Phaseolus acutifolius*] crosses with all varieties of tepary beans, but does not cross with other bean species listed in this chapter.
EASY TO SAVE SEEDS?	Yes
SEED TYPE REQUIRED FOR SEED SAVING:	Heirloom (open-pollinated) seeds (available at SeedRenaissance.com)
NUMBER OF VARIETIES AVAILABLE:	Many
LIFE SPAN OF PLANT:	Germination decreases after three years of ideal storage. Ideal storage means avoiding drastic temperature fluctuations by keeping seeds in a cool, dark, dry place.
LIFE SPAN OF SEED:	Germination decreases after five years of ideal storage. Ideal storage means avoiding drastic temperature fluctuations by keeping seeds in a cool, dark, dry place.
SEED MATURATION:	Allow seeds to dry fully on the plant in the garden or mature as long as possible in the garden, pull up the whole plant, roots and all, and dry in a cool dark place (like a garage), and then harvest seeds.
FLOWER TYPE:	Perfect
SEX TYPE:	Inbreeding

CROSSES WITH:	Necessity of isolation is debated but isolation is not commonly practiced.
POLLINATION TYPE:	Self-pollinating
SEEDS IN WHAT YEAR?	First year
ISOLATION DISTANCE:	None
SHATTERING RATE:	Slow
POPULATION MINIMUM:	10+ plants

SEED-CLEANING METHOD

Thresh by rubbing the dried pods together in a container to catch the seeds as they fall from the pods.

RECOMMENDED VARIETIES

Indian Woman Yellow

Of over two hundred varieties that I have trialed, this is the earliest to mature while still being hugely prolific. These are moderately sweet, green string beans, sometimes double stringed. They are very easy to grow, producing huge quantities of beans that are great for eating raw or cooked, frozen or canned. They will stay alive quite a while, as late as December, in a cold frame. This is also the best self-seeding bean I've ever found. These beans were given to me by a woman who attended a speech that I gave. The one company in the US that sold them has dropped them. SeedRenaissance.com is proud to be the only company in the world selling these beans, keeping the beans from extinction. The dried beans are a rustic yellow color. You can see pictures of them at SeedRenaissance.com.

Pioneer Pink-Eyed Beans

These beans have been saved from extinction by one family. I looked for this seed for a long time and had come to the conclusion that it was extinct. Over and over again, in my pioneer gardening research, I would read lists of vegetables the pioneers were growing, but often the only variety name they mentioned was pink-eyed beans. It is amazing how many pioneer accounts mention these beans. I'd looked everywhere for them, searched up and down, but had not been able to find any anywhere—even in seed banks. And then one day I gave a speech, and afterward, this beautiful tiny grandmother came up to me and asked if I had ever heard of pink-eyed beans.

"Yes, but I've searched everywhere for them and they are extinct," I said.

"I have some," she said. "And since I know you will grow them, I will give them to you."

I almost wept. I couldn't believe it. This wonderful woman got the seed from the last known family to grow it, and she gave it to me. Even though it was late June, I planted it immediately; thankfully, we had a late fall and these beans did very well in my garden before the frost in September. They are early bush beans, and they produce the largest common beans I've ever been able to grow—no wonder they were so popular with the pioneers. We cannot let them go extinct. They are too important. Available only at SeedRenaissance.com.

Dragon Tongue Bush Bean

I have learned over the years to test every seed I can get my hands on, because you never know when a seed will surprise you. To that end, I did a bean trial in my unheated geothermal greenhouse in January just to see what would happen—and lo and behold, this bean sprouted and grew. I have since tested it in the open garden in cold frames, where it also performs shockingly well. I have been told that this is actually an ancient Scandinavian bean, likely from Denmark, which is why it has this remarkable cold tolerance. This is also the second earliest bean to produce in side-by-side summer tests, and definitely the most beautiful bean I grow: a pale green bean with jagged purple streaks. It produces a lot of beans, and the beans are thick. They are not good for eating raw, but they are great when cooked. It also makes a good-sized shelling bean.

Broad Windsor Fava Bean

This remarkable fava (lima) bean has been grown in cold weather for centuries as a "hunger gap" food for both people and animals. It can be planted outside as soon as the soil can be worked in spring. You will be amazed to watch these beans grow even as temperatures dip below freezing at night, and they have been in full flower despite being covered with snow on many occasions in my garden. They produce huge, thick pods as summer is starting—when you are planting your common garden beans. The shelly beans are often the size of a quarter! These beans also do very well in the greenhouse when planted in January. This is a very old English heritage bean. It is great for eating (peel the inner shell off each fresh bean) and also an excellent way to help feed your chickens self-sufficiently. It's a reliable self-seeder, both in the backyard garden and in the greenhouse.

Fava beans

HOW TO SAVE SEEDS

Allow beans to dry on the vine. When they're dry, bring them indoors to finish open-air-drying for a couple of days before storing in a container. If you have bean weevils in your area (little bugs that burrow out of the dried beans, leaving the beans useless to use as seeds) follow the instructions in the chapter on peas in this book.

Bean chaff

Mixed beans

BEETS

SEED-CLEANING METHOD

Thresh and winnow.

RECOMMENDED VARIETIES

Albino Sugar Beets

Hundreds of you have tasted these beets at my classes, and thousands of you have read about me making sugar with these beets in my *Forgotten Skills* book. These seeds are difficult to find, which is why they are among the best sellers at SeedRenaisssance.com. If you have never tasted a sugar beet, you are in for a huge surprise—they taste like no other beet in the world. These pure white beets can be eaten just like any other beet—raw for a snack, raw in salads, baked, or cooked in soups and stews. This is one of my top ten must-have vegetables!

Chioggia Beets

These old Italian heirlooms are my favorite red beets in the world. Why? Because they don't bleed all over, they are stunning when cut open, and they are sweet and crisp. They don't taste at all like a traditional red beet. The flavor is a blend of sugar beet and traditional beet. They are great for eating raw as slices or for salads or cooking. I love these! Available at SeedRenaissance.com.

Golden Beets

These century-old American heirlooms are an orangey-gold color and have a mild, delicate flavor that stands out in roasted vegetable dishes. They look great in salads and served as a side dish. These are simply great! Available at SeedRenaissance.com.

SPECIES:	*Beta vulgaris*
EASY TO SAVE SEEDS?	Likely yes, if planting one variety per year within one species
SEED TYPE REQUIRED FOR SEED SAVING:	Heirloom (open-pollinated) seeds (available at SeedRenaissance.com)
NUMBER OF VARIETIES AVAILABLE:	Many
LIFE SPAN OF PLANT:	Biennial
LIFE SPAN OF SEED:	Germination decreases after six years of ideal storage. Ideal storage means avoiding drastic temperature fluctuations by keeping seeds in a cool, dark, dry place.
SEED MATURATION:	Allow seeds to dry fully on the plant in the garden or mature as long as possible in garden, pull up the whole plant—roots and all—, dry in a cool dark place, like a garage, and then harvest seeds.
FLOWER TYPE:	Perfect
SEX TYPE:	Outbreeding
CROSSES WITH:	All varieties of beets, sugar beets, mangels, and chard
POLLINATION TYPE:	Wind-pollinated
SEEDS IN WHAT YEAR?	Second year
ISOLATION DISTANCE:	Isolate different varieties by two miles
SHATTERING RATE:	Slow
POPULATION MINIMUM:	10+ plants

Mangels

After almost becoming extinct, there has been a small resurgence of interest in mangels. Mangels are a type of field beets that have been grown throughout the centuries as feed for horses, cows, oxen, donkeys and other livestock. They are a source of protein, are easy to store in winter, and grow large. Mangels were one of the most important sources of winter food for farmers who kept livestock over winter before the invention of modern baled hay or agricultural stores selling bags of winter livestock feed. Overwintering livestock animals in previous centuries was a very different enterprise than it is today. Historically, overwintering was done self-reliantly, meaning that the farmer had to grow all the food in summer that the animals would need once the ground was frozen. The way that animals are fed over winter today would have been considered luxurious or even wasteful in days gone by. In those days, the goal was to keep the animals alive through winter. It was considered normal for animals to lose weight in winter and fatten in summer as preparation for winter. Mangels cannot match the protein content of modern winter feeds, but they are still useful for anyone on small acreage who is trying to feed livestock as self-sufficiently as possible. Mangels are grown exactly like beets, but are harvested for human use only in the smallest stages. They quickly grow quite large and woody and are inedible to the human palate after the early stages of growth. It is not unusual for a single mangel beet to weigh twenty pounds or more, especially when grown in composted manure. Mangel seed is rare today. Few varieties remain, mostly because the number of farmers who use mangels as feed has dwindled to nearly zero. Today there are a few small farms and homesteads that grow mangels as feed supplements for livestock, and there has been a small increase in the number of people looking for mangel seed. It is available at SeedRenaissance.com.

HOW TO SAVE SEEDS

Beet seeds are harvested from second-year bulbs. Learning to harvest beet seeds begins with a caution: some beets might try to bolt (produce seed stalks) in the first year, especially if they are exposed to drought conditions. Don't allow seed to form from first-year bulbs, and do not harvest seed from first-year bulbs.

Why? Beets over the centuries have been "trained" by farmers to form a bulb for harvesting. Their natural inclination is to form seeds instead of a bulb. If you harvest seed from first-year plants, within a few generations of seed, you will have beets that produce only seeds and not root bulbs for eating. The roots will be skinny and useless—and then you have defeated the purpose of having the seed. To correctly produce beet seed, follow these steps:

Step 1:
Plant beet seeds and allow them to mature through the summer.

Step 2:
Carefully harvest the mature beets and select the best and most perfect specimens for seed saving. Caution: you can only save seed from one variety of beet. If you save two or more varieties, they will cross, which means your seed will be unstable. The traits that will be exhibited by unstable seeds are unpredictable. Unstable seed may produce seed like either parent or a combination of the two. Unstable seed may not continue to produce good bulbs after several generations, and you will not be able to predict the traits of the beets produced, including color, flavor, or size. For these reasons, be sure that you save beet bulbs from only one heirloom variety per year. The good news is that with ten seed plants, you will produce more than enough beet seed for several years of gardening, so you will be able to select a new variety for seed saving the next year.

Step 3:
Cut the leaves off the beets you have selected for seed saving. You may leave up to an inch of stem. Caution: do not cut the bulb of the beet itself. Even a small cut or scar may cause the beet to spoil in storage. Store these bulbs through winter in damp sand, sawdust, or pine shavings in a cool dark place such as a garage, basement cold room, or cellar. The temperature in your storage space must be cool, but cannot go below freezing or the beets will likely spoil. The beets will slowly produce edible leaves in the dark. Pick these leaves off monthly, as they take energy away from the bulb. Another caution: if you are also preserving beets for eating, make sure you don't mix up the beets you are keeping for eating with the beets you are keeping for seed, or you might eat your future seed-producing bulbs. This might seem like a minor concern, but if you are in the middle of making soup or roasted vegetables in December and you ask a child or spouse to "grab" some beets out of storage for you, and they bring the bulbs you have selected for seed saving without you realizing it, you have lost your potential for a seed crop.

Step 4:
In the spring of the second year, plant the saved bulbs in the outside garden in mid-spring. The bulbs will bolt (begin to form seed stalks) in early summer. The seeds are mature when the plants begin to dry up

and die. Caution: beet seeds are excellent at planting themselves. When dry, beet seeds are scattered by wind, rain, birds, and other hungry creatures. Once they are scattered, they are difficult to retrieve and may spoil if you try to save them because they are damp or muddy. Luckily, beet seeds tend to dry before the stems that hold them. To prevent scattering, harvest the seeds after they turn white, but before the stem fades from green to white (or red) and dies. To harvest the seed, lay a cloth or tarp on the ground under the plant. Wearing a leather glove, put your hand at the base of each beet stem and pull upward, knocking the seeds off the stem onto the tarp. Beet seeds are fairly large and woody. They are generally white in color and can be as large as a pea.

Step 5:
Once you have harvested the seeds, allow them to air-dry outside for several hours, up to a full day. This allows any bugs time to leave the seeds before you bring them indoors. However, while you are airing out your seeds outdoors, make sure they will not be exposed to water, wind, or birds.

Step 6:
Bring the seeds indoors for several days to dry. Dry them indoors to avoid weather, moisture, wind, and birds. Once seeds are completely dry, they can be stored in a paper, glass, or plastic container.

BROCCOLI

SEED-CLEANING METHOD

Thresh and winnow. When the seedpods are dry, rub them to release the seeds or uproot the plant carefully and hit it against the inside of a large box or plastic storage container to release and capture the seeds. Be careful when touching the dried plant in the garden, because the slightest shaking can cause hundreds of seeds to fall to the ground. You may want to place an old sheet on the ground under the plant before trying to harvest seeds or uproot the plant.

RECOMMENDED VARIETIES

Any heirloom variety with the shortest day count possible. Di Cicco is an heirloom favorite. Early purple sprouting broccoli is recommended for seed saving purposes, as explained below. Romanesco broccoli is also a fun spiral-shaped green variety, but it can be difficult to grow.

HOW TO SAVE SEEDS

Annual Method
Some early season broccolis can produce true seed in the first year, but attempting to save these seeds can be fraught because broccoli seeds, like most *Brassica* seeds, can take a long time to mature and

dry. Seedpods harvested before they mature and dry on the mother plant are rarely viable. Depending on where you live, you may need to extend the season, but building a cold frame large enough to house a flowering broccoli plant can be expensive and time consuming. Di Cicco is perhaps the best early season broccoli for backyard seed saving because it flowers in late August or early September, which may give you enough time to get naturally dried seedpods on the plant, depending on your autumn weather and how quickly the ground freezes. A few frosts will not stop the seeds from maturing on the plant, but if the ground freezes before the seeds are mature, you may lose the entire seed crop. The plant can be carefully dug up and transferred to a greenhouse for replanting to allow the seeds time to mature. Any seeds that dry on the mother plant while the plant is alive will be viable.

Biennial Method
Many Internet sources will tell you that to save broccoli seeds, you simply dig up the broccoli plant in the fall, store it for winter, and replant it in early spring. This advice comes only from writers with no personal experience. The truth is that broccoli does not store well overwinter. Most varieties are only viable in storage for about six weeks. For true seed saving, you

will need to overwinter the broccoli plant in a greenhouse. The best way to do this is to start the seeds in summer instead of spring, in pots. Allow the plants to grow in pots outside in the regular garden. You will need deep pots needed. Pots less than one gallon is size will likely be too small. After the first two or three frosts, move the pot into the greenhouse and allow the plant to continue flowering and seeding. Depending on your location and conditions in your winter greenhouse, the broccoli may go dormant for the winter and produce flowers and seeds in spring, or it may produce flowers and seeds in the winter. Any seeds that dry on the mother plant while the plant is alive will be viable.

Roguing

In botany, a "rogue" is any plant that is abnormal. Rogue plants should never be used for seed saving purposes, because the seeds may continue the abnormal traits of the mother plant. Only the best plants should be allowed to produce seeds. "Roguing" means pulling out any plants that exhibit inferior or unwanted traits for composting and not allowing them to go to seed.

Broccoli is difficult to save seed from and is not recommended for beginners. Saving broccoli seed is not generally practiced by home seed savers because of the difficulty level, evidenced by the five reasons listed below.

SPECIES:	*Brassica oleracea*
EASY TO SAVE SEEDS?	No Note: Birds will compete with you for the seeds.
SEED TYPE REQUIRED FOR SEED SAVING:	Heirloom (open-pollinated) seeds (available at SeedRenaissance.com).
NUMBER OF VARIETIES AVAILABLE:	Several
LIFE SPAN OF PLANT:	Biennial.
LIFE SPAN OF SEED:	Germination decreases after five years of ideal storage. Ideal storage means avoiding drastic temperature fluctuations by keeping seeds in a cool, dark, dry place.
SEED MATURATION:	Allow seeds to dry fully on the plant in the garden or mature as long as possible in garden, pull up the whole plant, roots and all, dry in a cool dark place, like a garage, and then harvest seeds.
FLOWER TYPE:	Perfect
SEX TYPE:	Outbreeding
CROSSES WITH:	All varieties of broccoli and all varieties of cabbage, brussels sprouts, cauliflower, collards, kale, and kohlrabi.
POLLINATION TYPE:	Insect-pollinated.
SEEDS IN WHAT YEAR?	Second year
ISOLATION DISTANCE:	One mile
SHATTERING RATE:	Quick
POPULATION MINIMUM:	10+ plants

1. To guarantee true and stable seed, professional broccoli seed saving is often labor intensive and expensive and can require artificially rooting stems and keeping them alive through winter in special greenhouses.

2. Broccoli plants cannot be harvested for eating if they are intended for seed saving. If the central head is harvested for eating, the secondary heads produce a lesser quality seed that is less likely to produce a central head and more likely to produce side shoots that mature over varying lengths of time.

3. Another reason that broccoli makes for difficult seed saving is because the *Brassica oleracea* species is promiscuous, and broccoli flowers will easily cross with all varieties of broccoli and all varieties of cabbage, brussels sprouts, cauliflower, collards, kale, and kohlrabi. You can have only one variety of any of these in flower in the garden at any given time, or they will cross and become unstable, meaning what grows from that seed will be unpredictable and susceptible to change each generation.

4. Broccoli, in particular, is almost immediately unlikely to produce central heads in any future generation if seed becomes unstable through promiscuous crossing.

5. When in flower, the entire *B. oleracea* species (all varieties of broccoli and all varieties of cabbage, brussels sprouts, cauliflower, collards, kale, and kohlrabi) requires a physical isolation of one mile from any other *B. oleracea* in flower in order to prevent cross-pollination. This isolation is difficult not only because few gardeners can control what flowers in a one-mile radius around their garden, but also because the entire *B. oleracea* species flowers early in spring and is highly attractive to bees at a time when there is not likely to be a lot of other vegetables in flower. This greatly increases the chances that, if there are other *B. oleracea* varieties in flower within that one-mile radius, the bees will cross the pollination just because they have so few food choices at this time of year.

If all of this has not deterred your desire to attempt to save broccoli seeds, there is one broccoli variety that offers the best chance for pure seed to backyard gardeners: early purple sprouting broccoli. This variety of broccoli is extremely winter hardy, which gives gardeners a chance of producing seed. However, it will still cross with any *B. oleracea* species within one mile. Despite this risk, I think it's worth it to try. Keep in mind, however, that you will have no way to know whether your seed is true until you grow it out. If your homegrown seed does not produce offspring exactly like the parents, you will know the seed was contaminated with neighboring pollen. Remember, however, that crossed phenotypes can take several generations of a seed line to appear in the traits of the plants. Saved seeds that appear stable in the first generation might prove to be unstable in the second and third generations.

Step 1:
Plant seeds of early purple sprouting broccoli directly in the garden in earliest autumn. Allow the plants to grow through autumn. You will need at least ten plants for a healthy gene pool.

Step 2:
The plants will tolerate light frosts. Before heavy frosts occur, cover the plants in a cold frame. Make sure that no part of the plant is in physical contact with the cold frame, or it may freeze and die. Plants should remain covered throughout the winter. I do not recommend trying to transplant to a greenhouse, because the stress of transplanting in the fall and transplanting back into the garden in spring can often hurt the plants.

Step 3:
In mid-spring (mid-March), remove the cold frame and allow the broccoli to naturally go to seed. Allow the seedpods to begin to dry and turn white on the stem, but harvest the seed before the pods begin to split open and scatter the seed. Test the seed for purity by growing it out. Never assume that homegrown broccoli seed is pure. Never attempt to sell broccoli or any other vegetable seed that you cannot guarantee is pure.

BRUSSELS SPROUTS

SEED-CLEANING METHOD
Thresh and winnow. When the seedpods are dry, rub them to release the seeds, or uproot the plant carefully and hit it against the inside of a large box or plastic storage container to release and capture the seeds. Be careful when touching the dried plant in the garden, because the slightest shaking can cause hundreds of seeds to fall to the ground. You may want to place an old sheet on the ground under the plant before trying to harvest seeds or uproot the plant.

RECOMMENDED VARIETIES
Any heirloom variety. There are no short-day-count varieties of brussels sprouts.

HOW TO SAVE SEEDS

Grow the brussels sprouts until the stalk is fully mature in late autumn. Do not harvest the sprouts. Instead, carefully dig up the whole plant, making sure to take as much of the large root as possible. Then "plant" this in a bucket of damp sand and store the whole plant in a dark garage that doesn't freeze, a cellar, or a basement cold room. In early to mid-spring, as soon as the ground can be worked deeply, transplant your brussels sprouts to the garden and let them establish new roots for two to three weeks. This is a lot of work, and the failure rate can be high, because not all mature brussels sprout plants will survive long enough in winter storage to be transplanted back into the garden in spring—and of those that do, some will not survive the transplant shock. If your winter climate is mild, you are much more likely to have success by leaving the plant in the garden over winter, but this is not possible in much of the US. To make matters even more difficult, brussels sprouts seed has low germination unless it is allowed to fully dry on the mother plant. If the seedpods are harvested too early, they will not mature. The last few days are critical, but it is also critical to harvest the seed before the pods split open and the seed drops out. Finally, some seed-borne diseases can be prevalent on brussels sprouts seeds, and indeed all *Brassicas*. These include black rot, black leg, and black leaf spot. To help reduce the chance of spreading these diseases on the seed, use a hot water treatment as described earlier in this book.

SPECIES:	*Brassica oleracea*
EASY TO SAVE SEEDS?	No
SEED TYPE REQUIRED FOR SEED SAVING:	Heirloom (open-pollinated) seeds (available at SeedRenaissance.com). *Note:* Birds will compete with you for the seeds.
LIFE SPAN OF PLANT:	Biennial
LIFE SPAN OF SEED:	Germination decreases after three years of ideal storage. Ideal storage means avoiding drastic temperature fluctuations by keeping seeds in a cool, dark, dry place.
SEED MATURATION:	Allow seeds to dry fully on the plant in the garden or mature as long as possible in the garden, pull up the whole plant, roots and all, dry in a cool dark place, like a garage, and then harvest seeds.
FLOWER TYPE:	Perfect
SEX TYPE:	Outbreeding
CROSSES WITH:	All varieties of brussels sprouts, as well as all varieties of broccoli, cabbage, cauliflower, collards, kale, and kohlrabi.
POLLINATION TYPE:	Insect
SEEDS IN WHAT YEAR?	Second year
ISOLATION DISTANCE:	One mile
SHATTERING RATE:	Quick
POPULATION MINIMUM:	10+ plants

CABBAGE

SEED-CLEANING METHOD

Thresh and winnow. When the seedpods are dry, rub them to release the seeds, or uproot the plant carefully and hit it against the inside of a large box or plastic storage container to release and capture the seeds. Be careful when touching the dried plant in the garden, because the slightest shaking can cause hundreds of seeds to fall to the ground. You may want to place an old sheet on the ground under the plant before trying to harvest seeds or uproot the plant.

Danish Ballhead Cabbage seeds

RECOMMENDED VARIETIES

Danish Ballhead cabbage, available at SeedRenaissance.com.

HOW TO SAVE SEEDS

Grow the cabbage until the head is full in late autumn, and then instead of harvesting the cabbage, carefully dig up

SPECIES:	*Brassica oleracea*
SEED TYPE REQUIRED FOR SEED SAVING:	Heirloom (open-pollinated) seeds (available at SeedRenaissance.com).
EASY TO SAVE SEEDS?	No *Note:* Birds will compete with you for the seeds.
LIFE SPAN OF PLANT:	Biennial
LIFE SPAN OF SEED:	Germination decreases after six years of ideal storage. Ideal storage means avoiding drastic temperature fluctuations by keeping seeds in a cool, dark, dry place.
SEED MATURATION:	Allow seeds to dry fully on the plant in the garden or mature as long as possible in the garden, pull up the whole plant, roots and all, dry in a cool dark place, like a garage, and then harvest seeds.
FLOWER TYPE:	Perfect
SEX TYPE:	Outbreeding
CROSSES WITH:	All varieties of cabbage and all varieties of broccoli, brussels sprouts, cauliflower, collards, kale, and kohlrabi.
POLLINATION TYPE:	Insect
SEEDS IN WHAT YEAR?	Second year
ISOLATION DISTANCE:	One mile
SHATTERING RATE:	Quick
POPULATION MINIMUM:	10+ plants

the whole plant, root and all, and then "plant" the cabbage root in a bucket of damp sand and store the whole plant in a dark garage that doesn't freeze, a cellar, or a basement cold room for winter use. In spring, as soon as the ground can be worked deeply, transplant this to the garden and let it establish new roots for two to three weeks. Then carefully and lightly cut an "x" shape into the cabbage head to encourage a seed stalk to grow out of the head. As you can tell, this is a lot of work, and the failure rate can be high, because not all cabbages will survive long enough in winter storage to be transplanted back into the garden in spring, and some will die from transplant shock.

Caution: If you harvest the cabbage head in summer or autumn, your cabbage plant may then produce flowers. You can save seeds from these flowers, but you run the risk that you will be breeding out the tendency of the plant to produce a head. Seeds saved from cabbage plants in the first year may not continue to produce cabbage heads in future generations. The first and second generations may produce smaller heads, and the head may just become leaves in the next generations. If you save seeds from cabbage plants in the first year, you should consider your seed to be experimental.

Washed cabbage seeds

CANTALOUPE/MELONS

SEED-CLEANING METHOD

Wash and air-dry indoors before storage. Seeds should never be dried in a machine or oven.

RECOMMENDED VARIETIES

Noir des Carmes cantaloupe, available from SeedRenaissance.com.

HOW TO SAVE SEEDS

Allow only one heirloom variety to flower at a time. In my garden, my neighbors on both sides grow cantaloupes in their gardens, but their cantaloupes have never crossed with my Noir des Carmes (as I discussed in my *More Forgotten Skills* book, there is some evidence that Noir des Carmes is self-pollinating, which cantaloupes are not supposed to be). Inevitably there are cantaloupes at the end of the season that end up rotting in the garden, especially if you grow a lot of cantaloupes like I do. Noir des Carmes is very good at self-seeding, especially in loamy soil. However, it is always a good idea to save the seeds from the cantaloupes you bring in the house to eat. After scooping them out of the melon, wash them in a sieve or colander, removing the largest chunks of fiber that may be attached to the seeds. Then air-dry the seeds indoors for a week or until they are completely dry. Store in a paper, glass, or plastic container in a cool, dry place. If you are not going to use the seeds within three years, freeze them. Keep in mind, however, that if neighbors within a half-mile are growing cantaloupe, they could be crossed in your garden by insects. You will not know for sure until you grow out the seeds to see what they produce.

SPECIES:	*Cucumis melo*
EASY TO SAVE SEEDS?	Likely yes, if planting one variety per year within one species. However, expect natural spontaneous abortion of 80 percent of female blossoms, despite natural or hand-pollination.
SEED TYPE REQUIRED FOR SEED SAVING:	Heirloom (open-pollinated) seeds (available at SeedRenaissance.com).
NUMBER OF VARIETIES AVAILABLE:	Dozens
LIFE SPAN OF PLANT:	Annual
LIFE SPAN OF SEED:	Germination decreases after one year of ideal storage. Ideal storage means avoiding drastic temperature fluctuations by keeping seeds in a cool, dark, dry place.
SEED MATURATION:	Seeds are ready for harvest when the fruit has begun to soften.
FLOWER TYPE:	Andromonoecious
SEX TYPE:	Outbreeding
CROSSES WITH:	All varieties of muskmelon, honeydew, casaba, Armenian cucumber, snake melon, Asian pickling melons, pocket melons, vine pomegranates, and vine peaches. Does not cross with watermelon.
POLLINATION TYPE:	Insect
SEEDS IN WHAT YEAR?	One year
ISOLATION DISTANCE:	One-half mile
SHATTERING RATE:	Not applicable
POPULATION MINIMUM:	3+ plants

CARROTS

SEED-CLEANING METHOD

Thresh and winnow. When the seed heads are dry, rub them to release the seeds, or uproot the plant carefully and hit it against the inside of a large box or plastic storage container to release and capture the seeds. Be careful when touching the dried plant in the garden, because the movement may cause some seeds to fall to the ground. You may want to place an old sheet on the ground under the plant before trying to harvest seeds or uproot the plant.

RECOMMENDED VARIETIES

Amarillo Carrot
These big yellow beauties are among the earliest maturing of all carrots and have a beautiful light yellow color and a crisp, sweet, bright flavor that I love. These hard-to-find seeds are available at SeedRenaissance .com.

Caleb's Color Carrot Mix
I like to grow and eat colorful food, so each year I grow a mixture of carrots that includes purple, red,

yellow, white and, yes, even some orange varieties. I select and blend this mixture myself. You can find it at SeedRenaissance.com.

HOW TO SAVE SEEDS

Saving backyard carrot seeds is a lesson in just how lucky we are to have the heirloom varieties that have been handed down to us through the generations. Why? Because it is nearly impossible for backyard gardeners to save true seed from backyard carrots for two reasons. First, because carrots are both wind- and insect-pollinated. Second, wild carrots grow all over the US and will easily cross-pollinate with garden carrots. Carrots can be hand-pollinated, but you would still need to keep the wind from cross-pollinating them. To make matters worse, cross-pollination is slow to show up in carrots. This means that if you save backyard carrot seeds and plant them, they may seem fine when grown out. But if you save seeds from the new crop of carrots, you will begin to notice the carrots turning white. This white coloring will get more pronounced with each generation. For this reason,

any garden carrot seed saving must be considered experimental at best. There is no reason not to try it. Just don't be surprised if, several generations down the line, the wild characteristics begin to become dominate. Carrots produce an umbel of seeds that should be allowed to dry in the garden. Once dried, they should be harvested fairly quickly so that birds and wind don't scatter the seeds to the earth. The seeds should be brought indoors to completely dry on a tray for several days. They can then be stored in a container in a cool, dry, dark place.

A friend of mine posted this question in a garden forum: "Can anybody tell me why the carrots that I have planted from seed are flowering in the first year? I thought they were a biennial."

Here is the answer I gave: In the wild, carrots often sprout in autumn, not spring. They produce a small, fibrous white root. The whole goal of this root is to overwinter so that the plant can produce a seed stalk the following summer. Humans have bred carrots that are best planted in spring, allowing them a full season of root development—so that the root can be used for food. This was done historically by refusing to let the spring-planted seeds form a seed stalk. The seed stalk was simply cut off. Over time, carrots were trained to produce a large root and seed in the second year. This way, roots in the first year could be harvested for food.

Carrot flowers

The carrots we have today were bred by our ancestors in this way to focus on root production in the first year and seed production in the second year, but a few will try to go to seed in the first year, especially if they are not given enough water or if they experience other environmental stress. The seed from these carrots should not be saved, because it encourages future generations of carrots that revert to feral, meaning they will focus on seed production instead of root production, making them useless as a food source. There are two things you can do to fight this. First, you can cut off the seed stalk as soon as you see it forming. This will force the carrot to refocus on root production instead of seed production. However, there are two problems with this. First, in hot, dry conditions, the root may try to re-bolt to form a seed stalk, and second, if the seed stalk was more than roughly six inches tall and you cut it, the plant may simply die instead of refocusing on root production.

The second thing you should do is just pull up the seed stalk and compost it before it can form seeds. This way there is no danger of encouraging bad carrot seed. Less than 5 percent of your carrots should bolt to seed stalks in the heat. If more than 5 percent bolt, it is highly likely that your seed is contaminated with wild carrot pollen.

SPECIES:	*Daucus carota sativus*
EASY TO SAVE SEEDS?	No
SEED TYPE REQUIRED FOR SEED SAVING:	Heirloom (open-pollinated) seeds (available at SeedRenaissance.com). Hybrid varieties (also called F1) are either sterile or genetically unstable, meaning the traits of resulting generations will be exponentially unpredictable. Selling home-saved hybrid seeds is illegal according to US law because the seeds are corporate owned. Genetically modified seeds are unstable, sterile, and illegal to save according to US law because the genetic design is corporate property. Note: Birds may compete with you for the seeds.
LIFE SPAN OF PLANT:	Biennial
LIFE SPAN OF SEED:	Germination decreases after two years of ideal storage. Ideal storage means avoiding drastic temperature fluctuations by keeping seeds in a cool, dark, dry place.
SEED MATURATION:	Allow seeds to dry fully on the plant in the garden, or mature as long as possible in garden, pull up the whole plant, roots and all, dry in a cool dark place, like a garage, and then harvest seeds.
FLOWER TYPE:	Perfect
SEX TYPE:	Outbreeding
CROSSES WITH:	All varieties of carrot and wild carrot. Wild carrots are called "white top" or Queen Anne's Lace and grow rampant all over the US, making pure carrot seeds difficult to save for the home grower.
POLLINATION TYPE:	Insect and wind
SEEDS IN WHAT YEAR?	Second year
ISOLATION DISTANCE:	One-half mile
SHATTERING RATE:	Slow
POPULATION MINIMUM:	10+ plants

CAULIFLOWER

SEED-CLEANING METHOD

Thresh and winnow. When the seedpods are dry, rub them to release the seeds, or uproot the plant carefully and hit it against the inside of a large box or plastic storage container to release and capture the seeds. Be careful when touching the dried plant in the garden, because the slightest shaking can cause hundreds of seeds to fall to the ground. You may want to place an old sheet on the ground under the plant before trying to harvest seeds or uproot the plant.

RECOMMENDED VARIETIES

Snowball cauliflower, available at SeedRenaissance.com.

HOW TO SAVE SEEDS

Annual Method

Like broccoli, some early season cauliflowers can produce true seed in the first year, but attempting this can be fraught, because cauliflower seeds, like most *Brassica* seeds, can take a long time to mature and dry. Seedpods harvested before they mature and dry on the mother plant are rarely viable. Depending on where you live, you may need to extend the season, but building a cold frame large enough to house a flowering cauliflower plant can be expensive and time consuming. A few frosts will not stop the seeds from maturing on the plant, but if the ground freezes before the seeds are mature, you may lose the entire seed crop. The plant can be carefully dug up and transferred to a greenhouse for replanting to allow the seeds time to mature. Any seeds that dry on the mother plant while the plant is alive will be viable.

SPECIES:	*Brassica oleracea*
EASY TO SAVE SEEDS?	No
SEED TYPE REQUIRED FOR SEED SAVING:	Heirloom (open-pollinated) seeds (available at SeedRenaissance.com).
NUMBER OF VARIETIES AVAILABLE:	Several
LIFE SPAN OF PLANT:	Biennial
LIFE SPAN OF SEED:	Germination decreases after two years of ideal storage. Ideal storage means avoiding drastic temperature fluctuations by keeping seeds in a cool, dark, dry place.
SEED MATURATION:	Allow seeds to dry fully on the plant in the garden or mature as long as possible in garden, pull up the whole plant, roots and all, dry in a cool dark place, like a garage, and then harvest seeds.
FLOWER TYPE:	Perfect
SEX TYPE:	Outbreeding
CROSSES WITH:	All varieties of cauliflower and all varieties of broccoli, brussels sprouts, cabbage, collards, kale, and kohlrabi.
POLLINATION TYPE:	Insect
SEEDS IN WHAT YEAR?	Second year
ISOLATION DISTANCE:	One mile
SHATTERING RATE:	Quick
POPULATION MINIMUM:	10+ plants

Biennial Method

Many Internet sources will tell you that to save cauliflower seeds (indeed, all *brassica oleracea* seeds), you simply dig up the cauliflower plant in the fall, store it for winter, and replant it in early spring. This advice comes only from writers with no firsthand experience. The truth is that cauliflower, like broccoli, does not store well over winter. Most varieties are only viable in storage for about six weeks. For true seed saving, you will need to overwinter the cauliflower plant in a greenhouse. The best way to do this is to start the seeds in summer instead of spring, in pots. Allow the plants to grow in pots outside, in the regular garden. Deep pots are needed. Pots less than one gallon in size will likely be too small. After the first two or three frosts, move the pot into the greenhouse and allow the plant to continue flowering and seeding. Depending on your location and conditions in your winter greenhouse, the cauliflower may go dormant for the winter and produce flowers and seeds in spring, or it may produce flowers and seeds in the winter. Any seeds that dry on the mother plant while the plant is alive will be viable.

Roguing

In botany, a "rogue" is any plant that is abnormal. Rogue plants should never be used for seed saving purposes, because the seeds may continue the abnormal traits of the mother plant. Only the best plants should be allowed to produce seeds. Roguing means that any plants that exhibit inferior or unwanted traits are pulled out for composting and are not allowed to go to seed. Cauliflower can be difficult to grow because it likes cool weather. Hot weather can cause all kinds of abnormal behavior in the plants, ranging from plants that produce no heads to heads that are deformed. None of these should be used for seed saving.

CELERY

SPECIES:	*Apium graveolens*
EASY TO SAVE SEEDS?	Likely yes, if planting one variety per year within one species.
SEED TYPE REQUIRED FOR SEED SAVING:	Heirloom (open-pollinated) seeds (available at SeedRenaissance.com).
NUMBER OF VARIETIES AVAILABLE:	Several
LIFE SPAN OF PLANT:	Biennial
LIFE SPAN OF SEED:	Germination decreases after six years of ideal storage. Ideal storage means avoiding drastic temperature fluctuations by keeping seeds in a cool, dark, dry place.
SEED MATURATION:	Allow seeds to dry fully on the plant in the garden or mature as long as possible in garden, pull up the whole plant, roots and all, dry in a cool dark place, like a garage, and then harvest seeds.
FLOWER TYPE:	Perfect
SEX TYPE:	Outbreeding
CROSSES WITH:	All varieties of celery, celeriac (also called celery root), and smallage, which is wild celery.
POLLINATION TYPE:	Insect
ISOLATION DISTANCE:	Three mile
SHATTERING RATE:	Quick
POPULATION MINIMUM:	10+ plants

SEED-CLEANING METHOD

Thresh and winnow. When the seedpods are dry, rub them to release the seeds, or uproot the plant carefully and hit it against the inside of a large box or plastic storage container to release and capture the seeds. Be careful when touching the dried plant in the garden, because the slightest shaking can cause hundreds of seeds to fall to the ground. You may want to place an old sheet on the ground under the plant before trying to harvest seeds or uproot the plant.

RECOMMENDED VARIETIES

Calypso celery and varieties listed at SeedRenaissance.com.

HOW TO SAVE SEEDS

Saving celery seed is a two-year process. There are two methods.

First method

In the first year, plant celery and allow it to mature. In autumn, before the ground freezes, trim the celery back, leaving only one to two inches of stems. Cover with eight to twelve inches of loose straw, and then top the straw with a bag of yard leaves. Let the leaves remain in the bag, and simply set the bag on top of the straw as a weight. Or cover the straw with a cold frame or row cover. The goal is to protect the roots of the celery plants over winter. In spring, uncover totally when the ground unfreezes, and allow the celery plant to grow, produce flower stalks, and go to seed. The seed umbels can be harvested as soon as they are dry. Do not wait long or they will naturally break open and shatter, and the seed will be lost. This method is easier because it does not require storing the plants indoors over winter, and the risk of losing the plants in spring is lower. However, the risk of this method is that a creature (vole, mole, or mouse, for example) can find the plant under the straw in winter and eat it. Such a creature may even eat the roots, killing the plant. Allow the seeds to dry on the plant before harvesting.

Second method

In autumn, dig up your celery plants. Trim them so that only one to two inches of stems remain. "Plant" them in damp sand, with just the roots covered, leaving the trimmed top open to the air. Store in a dry, dark place that will not freeze, such as a cellar or an unheated, dark garage. In spring, when the soil can be worked, transplant back to the open garden. Allow the celery plant to grow, produce flower stalks, and go to seed. The seed umbels can be harvested as soon as they are dry. Do not wait long or they will naturally break open and shatter, and the seed will be lost. This method is not my favorite, because even if the plants store perfectly, some are likely to go into transplant shock when moved outside in spring, and they can die from this shock. Allow the seeds to dry on the plant before harvesting.

CHINESE CABBAGE

SEED-CLEANING METHOD

Thresh and winnow. When the seedpods are dry, rub them to release the seeds, or uproot the plant carefully and hit it against the inside of a large box or plastic storage container to release and capture the seeds. Be careful when touching the dried plant in the garden, because the slightest shaking can cause hundreds of seeds to fall to the ground. You may want to place an old sheet on the ground under the plant before trying to harvest seeds or uproot the plant.

RECOMMENDED VARIETIES

Chinese Michihili Cabbage, available at SeedRenaissance.com.

HOW TO SAVE SEEDS

Chinese cabbage plants go to seed easily and quickly in hot weather. There is some controversy over whether these plants should be allowed to go to seed in the first year and whether loose-leaf cabbages should be harvested for seed. If you only like to harvest and head solid heads of Chinese cabbage, you will need the long, cool growing season required to produce these kinds of heads. Those heads should be dug up, root and all, in fall, "planted" in damp sand or damp pine shavings in a bucket, and stored over winter in a cool, dry, dark place. Roots must remain moist but not damp enough to encourage rot. In spring, when the ground can be worked, transplant back outside. The plant may need protection on cold spring nights. The cabbage head may need to be cut with a deep "x" shape to encourage a seed stalk to form. Seeds should be harvested once they dry on the stem. Seedpods will shatter quickly once dry, so harvest as soon as they are dry. Chinese cabbage can be allowed to go to seed in the first year and as loose-leaf plants. Genetically, however, these plants are likely to produce future generations that increasingly want to seed in the first year and may be less likely to produce a solid head if the plant that produced the seed never produced a firm, solid head. For me, having a solid head is not a goal, so it is not an issue, especially because my cool season is too short to produce solid Chinese cabbage heads anyway.

SPECIES:	*Brassica rapa*
EASY TO SAVE SEEDS?	Likely yes, if planting one variety per year within one species. *Note*: Birds will compete with you for the seeds.
SEED TYPE REQUIRED FOR SEED SAVING:	Heirloom (open-pollinated) seeds (available at SeedRenaissance.com).
NUMBER OF VARIETIES AVAILABLE:	Several
LIFE SPAN OF PLANT:	Ideally biennial, but may produce seed annually.
LIFE SPAN OF SEED:	Germination decreases after one year of ideal storage. Ideal storage means avoiding drastic temperature fluctuations by keeping seeds in a cool, dark, dry place.
SEED MATURATION:	Allow seeds to dry fully on the plant in the garden or mature as long as possible in garden, pull up the whole plant, roots and all, dry in a cool dark place, like a garage, and then harvest seeds.
FLOWER TYPE:	Perfect
SEX TYPE:	Outbreeding
CROSSES WITH:	All varieties of Chinese cabbage and all varieties of turnips, broccoli raab, and Chinese mustards including mizuna.
POLLINATION TYPE:	Insect
SEEDS IN WHAT YEAR?	Second year. May produce seed in the first year.
ISOLATION DISTANCE:	One mile
SHATTERING RATE:	Quick
POPULATION MINIMUM:	10+ plants

COLLARDS

SPECIES:	*Brassica oleracea*
EASY TO SAVE SEEDS?	Likely yes, if planting one variety per year within one species. *Note:* Birds will compete with you for the seeds.
SEED TYPE REQUIRED FOR SEED SAVING:	Heirloom (open-pollinated) seeds (available at SeedRenaissance.com).
NUMBER OF VARIETIES AVAILABLE:	Several
LIFE SPAN OF PLANT:	Biennial
LIFE SPAN OF SEED:	Germination decreases after six years of ideal storage. Ideal storage means avoiding drastic temperature fluctuations by keeping seeds in a cool, dark, dry place.
SEED MATURATION:	Allow seeds to dry fully on the plant in the garden or mature as long as possible in the garden, pull up the whole plant, roots and all, dry in a cool dark place, like a garage, and then harvest seeds.
FLOWER TYPE:	Perfect
SEX TYPE:	Outbreeding
CROSSES WITH:	All varieties of collards, as well as all varieties of broccoli, brussels sprouts, cauliflower, cabbage, kale, and kohlrabi.
POLLINATION TYPE:	Insect
SEEDS IN WHAT YEAR?	Second year
ISOLATION DISTANCE:	One mile
SHATTERING RATE:	Quick
POPULATION MINIMUM:	10+ plants

SEED-CLEANING METHOD

Thresh and winnow. When the seedpods are dry, rub them to release the seeds, or uproot the plant carefully and hit it against the inside of a large box or plastic storage container to release and capture the seeds. Be careful when touching the dried plant in the garden, because the slightest shaking can cause hundreds of seeds to fall to the ground. You may want to place an old sheet on the ground under the plant before trying to harvest seeds or uproot the plant.

RECOMMENDED VARIETIES

Vates collards, an old variety available at SeedRenaissance.com.

HOW TO SAVE SEEDS

For long-term viability, save seeds from no less than ten plants. Collards throw their seeds in mid to late summer. Only one variety of this species may be in flower at a time. The pods shatter and release the seed to the ground and the birds. The seeds germinate on their own in about four weeks. If you want to thin the number of plants, keep the earliest, largest, and most perfect plants and pull out the smaller ones. Seeds should be gathered just as the pods begin to turn tan in color but before they shatter and open. Seeds may be collected from the ground if needed, as long as they are dry. Crush the pods with gloved hands to release the seeds into a container. Store in a cool, dry, dark place.

Collard flowers

Collard pods

Immature Collard seeds

CORN

SPECIES:	*Zea mays*. Includes sweet corn, fodder corn (corn for animal feed), and popcorn.
EASY TO SAVE SEEDS?	No
SEED TYPE REQUIRED FOR SEED SAVING:	Heirloom (open-pollinated) seeds (available at SeedRenaissance.com).
NUMBER OF VARIETIES AVAILABLE:	Several
LIFE SPAN OF PLANT:	Annual
LIFE SPAN OF SEED:	Germination decreases after three years of ideal storage. Ideal storage means avoiding drastic temperature fluctuations by keeping seeds in a cool, dark, dry place.
SEED MATURATION:	Allow seeds to dry fully on the plant in the garden.
FLOWER TYPE:	Monoecious
SEX TYPE:	Outbreeding
CROSSES WITH:	All varieties of sweet corn, fodder corn, popcorn, and genetically modified corn.
POLLINATION TYPE:	Wind
SEEDS IN WHAT YEAR?	First year
ISOLATION DISTANCE:	Two to five miles depending on variety. Extremely susceptible to inbreeding depression. Block pattern growing increases pollination.
SHATTERING RATE:	Not applicable
POPULATION MINIMUM:	Debated. To truly remove potential for inbreeding depression, I recommend 1,000+ plants.

SEED-CLEANING METHOD

Thresh by rubbing two dried cobs together to loosen and remove the seeds. Place a bowl under the cobs to catch the seeds. Wear gloves, because the dried cobs can quickly damage bare hands.

Modern corn is one of the most fragile vegetables in the world. As you begin to learn about the history of growing corn and saving corn seed, you begin to learn just how vulnerable this species is. Wild corn, which can still be found in South America, resembles a dwarf version of broomcorn and does not have ears. Corn is perhaps the most malleable plant in the garden, and I encourage everyone to try to save corn seed so you can see first-hand how fragile the world's seed stocks are. Because corn is wind-pollinated and does not self-pollinate, saving pure corn seed was difficult before the invention of hybrid, and then genetically modified, corn. Today, it is increasingly looking like keeping pure heirloom corn seed might be impossible in the long term, which would be a huge loss of centuries of work. Imagine a world where there is no public domain corn seed left, a world where the only corn seed in existence is patented, corporate-owned, and genetically modified or hybrid so that it does not produce true seed. This could be true within five years. Why? Because corn is wind-pollinated, so no one can control the spread of genetically modified and hybridized genes.

RECOMMENDED VARIETIES

Stowell's Evergreen Sweet Corn
This is my favorite corn ever, and it's called "evergreen" for a reason. This is one of the oldest original sweet corn varieties in America, and it was always used by homesteaders and pioneers to extend the season—it stays sweet on the stalk for weeks for extended fresh picking. If you want to use it for winter, there are two options for using this rare, unusual corn. As detailed in my first *Forgotten Skills* book, just before the first frost of fall, you can pull the entire stalk up—roots and all—and hang it upside down in your garage or cellar. Treated like this, the corn will stay sweet and ripe for four to eight weeks. This is not a rumor—I've tested it! The second way this corn used to be used is by boiling. You can cut it up when it's ripe, then dry it, store it, and boil it

in milk in winter until it is plump and tender again. I've also done this, and it tastes great. It tastes exactly like the boiled corn my great-grandmother used to serve at her dinner table. Very nostalgic for me. I love this corn and grow it every year. This is yellow corn.

Country Gentleman

This white sweet corn is the heirloom variety that comes closest to the sugary flavor of the genetically modified corn that I am strongly opposed to and that will not grow in my garden. Country Gentleman is packed with rows of small white juicy kernels that are tender and flavorful when cooked. Yum!

Golden Bantam Sweet Corn

This yellow sweet corn has that old-fashioned true corn taste that is so often missing from the genetically modified corn today. If you were ever lucky enough to have fresh corn out of your great-grandmother's garden, this is what that corn tasted like (and it very

well could be this corn that your great-grandmother was growing!)

HOW TO SAVE SEEDS

Saving truly pure seed from corn is tricky and difficult work for backyard seed savers. The tassels at the top of the plant produce pollen. Corn plants do not accept their own pollen and must be pollinated by another plant. Floating on the wind for miles, this pollen pollinates each individual silk on an ear of corn—one silk pollinates one kernel of corn. Any corn within five miles can pollinate the corn in your garden. Isolation by distance is nearly impossible for practical purposes, because who can control all corn within five miles of their garden?

In a blog post from December 9, 2013, titled "Preventing GMO Contamination in Your Open-Pollinated Corn," the experts at SeedSavers revealed something startling. Corn may be both easier and more difficult to keep pure than previously imagined.

Corn can be hand-pollinated, but this is labor-intensive work that must be done with precision. Each ear of corn needs to be covered with a bag before any silks emerge. The tassels must be bagged too, tightly. These bags are then used to pollinate the ears. After hearing this, you might begin to wonder how corn was kept pure historically. Like all vegetables, the answer is isolation. Corn was isolated by distance, and the farther the distance, the less likely it is that unwanted corn pollen will pollute your corn. SeedSavers reports that the 1917 book *Corn Among the Indians of the Upper Missouri*, written by George Will, tells us that fourteen distinct corn varieties were maintained by the Mandan Nation of North Dakota, who kept the corn pure "by growing each variety 'a couple hundred yards' apart, and by careful ear selection for their seed corn."

Startling indeed. So is there hope that corn can be kept pure by such small isolation distances?

SeedSavers also reports modern research showing that corn varieties isolated by six hundred feet usually have less than 1 percent cross-pollination. A study done by Ohio State University showed that "cross-pollination could not be limited to 0.1% consistently even with isolation distances of 1640 feet."[1]

The 890-acre SeedSavers farm in Decorah, Iowa, is surrounded by genetically modified cornfields, because that is what farmers in Iowa and most of the nation grow. In 2013, SeedSavers grew a large

Country Gentleman

planting of a rare corn called "Hjerleid Blue," an heirloom blue sweet corn grown by the Hjerleid family of Wisconsin since the 1940s. They felt the field of corn was too large to be hand-pollinated. The field was 2,300 feet from any other cornfield, and there was forest and elevation changes between the Hjerleid Blue and the nearest corn. SeedSavers goes into a lot of detail about what I'm about to say, but I'm going to simplify it to say this: because the blue color of Hjerleid is genetically recessive, any contamination would appear as yellow kernels of corn.

"A kernel of 'Hjerleid Blue' pollinated by GMO pollen would be non-wrinkled and have a yellow endosperm—it would easily stand out amongst its peers," SeedSavers wrote. "We thought that growing 'Hjerleid Blue' in our isolated, buffered garden would be sufficient to prevent any cross-pollination with neighboring GMO corn. We were wrong."

Six ears of the corn contained GMO-contaminated kernels. This gene pollution is less than a tenth of one percent of the crop of Hjerleid they grew. But if those kernels were planted, the genetic pollution would increase exponentially through future generations.

Of even greater concern is that according to federal law, it is legal to label this low level of contamination as "non-GMO" despite the fact that the seed would increase contamination in future generations. The government considers this level of GMO genetic pollution to be "acceptable," even though those

of us who are concerned about the spread of GMO would never find it "acceptable." What this means is that corn that is legally "non-GMO" is, in fact, capable of contaminating local crops with genetically modified pollen.

"For the purposes of saving seed, any GMO contamination is unacceptable because the contamination will increase exponentially in each successive generation," says SeedSavers.

Even more concerning is this: "Had we grown an historic yellow dent corn in that orchard garden, we never would have known that we had introduced GMO genes into the population because it would not have been visually apparent."

I don't mean to be alarmist, but there is only one scientific conclusion we can draw from this. In practical terms, any yellow corn seed can legally be—and likely is—contaminated with some level of GMO pollination, whether it is labeled non-GMO or not.

"The Midwestern summer air is awash with GMO pollen," says Seedsavers. "Corn-belt seed savers who want to ensure they eliminate all GMO contamination may want to learn to hand-pollinate their corn, or grow varieties where GMO contamination is visually apparent, such as white or blue corn."[2]

I'm going to go a step further. GMO corn is widespread. Most farms grow it. It is prevalent all over the contiguous United States. Some garden corn varieties are also GMO. Keeping it out of the garden might be as impossible as keeping the wind out of the garden.

HAND-POLLINATION OF CORN

For an expert tutorial of how to hand-pollinate corn, type "seed savers corn hand pollination" into a search engine and find the seedsavers.org tutorial, or go to:

https://exchange.seedsavers.org/storage/ FF4218E1-7760-43C1-AFAF-0EE4C4658BFF.pdf.

NOTES

1. Peter Thomison and Allen Geyer, "Managing 'Pollen Drift' to Minimize Contamination of Non-GMO Corn," *Ohioline*, http://ohioline.osu.edu/factsheet/agf-1533.

2. Tor Janson, "Preventing GMO Contamination in Your Open-Pollinated Corn," Seed Savers Blog, December 9, 2013, http://blog.seedsavers.org/blog/preventing-gmo-contamination-in-your-open-pollinated-corn.

CUCUMBER

SEED-CLEANING METHOD

Wash and air-dry indoors before storage. Seeds should never be dried in a machine or oven.

RECOMMENDED VARIETIES

Marketmore
My favorite pickling cucumber—it's green, straight, sweet, prolific, and fast growing. Plant directly in the garden after all danger of frost.

Poona Kheera
This is a sweet, never bitter yellow cucumber that is perfect for fresh eating and salads. You will love the flavor!

HOW TO SAVE SEEDS

If you intend to save seeds, you must grow only one variety of cucumber or they will cross—and they may cross with your neighbor's cucumbers anyway. Let the cucumbers mature and stay on the vine until they begin to lose their color and soften. When they are soft you may harvest the seeds. Scrape the seeds from the cucumber. Wash the seeds, removing any pulp, and let them air dry indoors for at least a week before storing in a container.

Cuke flower

Poona cucumber

SPECIES:	*Cucumis sativus*
EASY TO SAVE SEEDS?	Likely yes, if planting one variety per year within one species.
SEED TYPE REQUIRED FOR SEED SAVING:	Heirloom (open-pollinated) seeds (available at SeedRenaissance.com).
NUMBER OF VARIETIES AVAILABLE:	Many
LIFE SPAN OF PLANT:	Annual
LIFE SPAN OF SEED:	Germination decreases after ten years of ideal storage. Ideal storage means avoiding drastic temperature fluctuations by keeping seeds in a cool, dark, dry place.
SEED MATURATION:	Seeds are ready to harvest when the cucumber begins to turn soft (and often has become discolored).
FLOWER TYPE:	Andromonoecious
SEX TYPE:	Outbreeding
CROSSES WITH:	All varieties of cucumbers, including gherkins. Does not cross with West Indian gherkins, Armenian cucumbers, snake melons, or serpent gourds.
POLLINATION TYPE:	Insect-pollinated
SEEDS IN WHAT YEAR?	First year
ISOLATION DISTANCE:	One-half mile
SHATTERING RATE:	Not applicable
POPULATION MINIMUM:	10+ plants

EGGPLANT

SPECIES:	*Solanum melongena*
EASY TO SAVE SEEDS?	Yes
SEED TYPE REQUIRED FOR SEED SAVING:	Heirloom (open-pollinated) seeds (available at SeedRenaissance .com).
NUMBER OF VARIETIES AVAILABLE:	Many
LIFE SPAN OF PLANT:	Annual
LIFE SPAN OF SEED:	Germination decreases after seven years of ideal storage. Ideal storage means avoiding drastic temperature fluctuations by keeping seeds in a cool, dark, dry place.
SEED MATURATION:	Seeds are ready to harvest when the fruit begins to soften toward rotting.
FLOWER TYPE:	Perfect
SEX TYPE:	Inbreeding
CROSSES WITH:	All varieties of eggplant.
POLLINATION TYPE:	Self-pollinating. Occasionally insect-pollinating.
SEEDS IN WHAT YEAR?	First year
ISOLATION DISTANCE:	Fifty feet
SHATTERING RATE:	Not applicable.
POPULATION MINIMUM:	10+ plants

SEED-CLEANING METHOD

Wash and air dry indoors before storage. Seeds should never be dried in a machine or oven.

HOW TO SAVE SEEDS

Even though eggplants are self-fertile, there is some small natural crossing over time that keeps the plants genetically healthy, so seeds should be saved from groups of ten plants or larger. Seeds can be saved from a single plant, but those seeds may demonstrate weak genetics over future generations. It is critical, when saving eggplant seeds, to allow the eggplant fruits to remain on the vine as long as possible. Bring the fruits inside only when the plants have begun to die.

Allow the fruits to sit and "mature" indoors for two to three weeks after harvest or until the eggplant begins to rot. Like squash seeds, eggplant seeds reach their highest viability only when the fruit over-ripens and begins to rot. Seeds gathered from eggplants that were not overripe will have low germination or may not be viable at all. In her seminal book *Seed to Seed*, Suzanne Ashworth suggests that the easiest method for harvesting eggplant seeds is to grate the bottom of the eggplant and then squeeze or rub the grated flesh in large bowl of water. Viable seeds will sink to the bottom, and the grated flesh and unripe seeds will float and can be discarded or fed to the chickens. Seeds can also be picked out of the eggplant fruit by hand.

GARLIC

SPECIES:	Allium sativum
EASY TO SAVE SEEDS?	Likely yes, if planting one variety per year within one species.
SEED TYPE REQUIRED FOR SEED SAVING:	Heirloom (open-pollinated) seeds (available at SeedRenaissance.com).
NUMBER OF VARIETIES AVAILABLE:	Many
LIFE SPAN OF PLANT:	Biennial
LIFE SPAN OF SEED:	Germination of cloves decreases after one year of ideal storage. Ideal storage means avoiding drastic temperature fluctuations by keeping seeds in a cool, dark, dry place.
SEED MATURATION:	When the stem is dry in autumn, the cloves are ready for storage.
FLOWER TYPE:	Not applicable
SEX TYPE:	Not applicable
CROSSES WITH:	Should not be allowed to flower for seed saving purposes. Propagate by saving cloves. Does not cross with elephant garlic.
POLLINATION TYPE:	None
SEEDS IN WHAT YEAR?	Second year
ISOLATION DISTANCE:	None
SHATTERING RATE:	Not applicable
POPULATION MINIMUM:	Not applicable

SEPARATING CLOVES

One head of garlic is comprised of many cloves. Break the dried cloves apart without damaging the individual cloves. When planted, one clove will grow to become a new head of garlic.

Garlic varieties are divided into hard-neck types and soft-neck types. Hard-neck garlic is grown in cold northern climates and forms a seed stalk. Soft-neck types are grown in mild climates. Soft-neck types do not store well and typically cannot overwinter in northern gardens.

There are two ways to propagate backyard garlic: the perennial method and the annual method.

Perennial Method

Plant the garlic cloves in the fall. By the fall of the second year, they will have multiplied to create a head of cloves. Some garlic varieties are hardier than others. If you live in an area with bitter winter temperatures, choose the hardiest varieties. Elephant garlic, which is not actually garlic but a member of the leek family, is particularly hardy. Elephant garlic is unlikely to need cover in the winter even in the north, but it will benefit from cover with a cloche, cold frame, or a foot-deep layer of hay, straw or leaves. Some true garlic may need some kind of cover each winter. The bulbs should be covered as described above before the ground freezes for winter, and you should uncover them as soon as the ground around the cover thaws in early spring. The bulbs should be harvested by leaving some part of the clove and roots in the ground, which is easier with elephant garlic. True garlic will be easier to harvest partially in the third year, when the bulbs are expanding.

Annual Method

Heads of true garlic and elephant garlic are broken into individual cloves for planting in the fall. These cloves multiply to produce heads of garlic in summer, and these heads are harvested when the garlic dries in the garden. The heads are broken up, and the best cloves are saved for planting again in the fall, while the rest are eaten.

WHEN TO PLANT

In northern climates, both elephant and true garlic is planted in autumn, generally in mid-October. In mild southern climates, garlics are planted any time in winter.

RECOMMENDED VARIETIES

Any heirloom variety. There are differences in flavor in most varieties, some being hotter, some being milder, some being more intense in aroma and flavor. Elephant garlic is milder by nature and is generally not used medicinally.

HOW TO SAVE SEEDS

Garlic is reproduced from bulbs, not seeds. If garlic attempts to flower, cut the flower stalk to prevent flowers from forming, because flowers can cause a shriveled bulb.

KALE

SEED-CLEANING METHOD

Thresh and winnow. When the seedpods are dry, rub them to release the seeds, or uproot the plant carefully and hit it against the inside of a large box or plastic storage container to release and capture the seeds. Be careful when touching the dried plant in the garden, because the slightest shaking can cause hundreds of seeds to fall to the ground. You may want to place an old sheet on the ground under the plant before trying to harvest seeds or uproot the plant.

RECOMMENDED VARIETIES

Dwarf blue Siberian kale, available from SeedRenaissance.com. This variety does not cross with traditional kale or brassicas, and is self-seeding, making it ideal for perennial gardens.

HOW TO SAVE SEEDS

Kale plants go to flower in mid-spring and produce seedpods in early summer. The pods will naturally break open when they are dry, and the seed will

Kale flowers

SPECIES:	Two species are commonly grown in the garden.
	Common kales [*Brassica oleracea*] cross with all varieties of kale, as well as all varieties of broccoli, brussels sprouts, cauliflower, collards, cabbage, and kohlrabi. Does not cross with Siberian kales (*Brassica napus* species).
	Siberian kales [*Brassica napus*] are also called Swedes or Swede turnips. They cross with other varieties of rutabaga, as well as all varieties of Siberian kale, Hanover salad and oilseed rape (sometimes just called rape or rapa). May also cross with fodder turnips. Does not cross with common kales (*Brassica oleracea*).
EASY TO SAVE SEEDS?	Likely yes, if planting one variety per year within one species.
	Note: Birds will compete with you for the seeds.
SEED TYPE REQUIRED FOR SEED SAVING:	Heirloom (open-pollinated) seeds (available at SeedRenaissance.com).
NUMBER OF VARIETIES AVAILABLE:	Many
LIFE SPAN OF PLANT:	Biennial
LIFE SPAN OF SEED:	Germination decreases after four years of ideal storage. Ideal storage means avoiding drastic temperature fluctuations by keeping seeds in a cool, dark, dry place.
SEED MATURATION:	Allow seeds to dry fully on the plant in the garden, or mature as long as possible in garden, pull up the whole plant, roots and all, and dry in a cool dark place, like a garage, and then harvest seeds.
FLOWER TYPE:	Perfect
SEX TYPE:	*Brassica napus* is inbreeding. *Brassica oleracea* is outbreeding
POLLINATION TYPE:	Insect

spill to the ground. If you want the plants to self-propagate, you don't need to do anything. Simply let the seeds spill to the ground, and they will self-germinate in wet weather. In my garden, the seeds move up to six feet a year. If you want them to fall in a certain place or move in a certain direction, you can harvest the seeds and scatter them yourself. If you want to save seeds for another year or control where they fall, keep an eye on the plants as they begin to dry down. As soon as one pod breaks open, pull up the whole plants, roots and all, and allow them to cure in the sun or shade for three to four days.

The best way to do this is by using an old bed sheet. The plants will be four to five feet tall as they begin to dry and produce seed. Place the pulled-up plants in the center of an old bed sheet and then tie the corners of the sheet to create a loose bundle. Allow the bundle to dry in the open air, in sun or shade, for three to four days. The bundle can be stored in a dry place and left for several weeks if needed. When you get ready to thresh the seed, some of it will have fallen out of the pods and will be captured on the bottom of the sheet bundle. Open the bundle carefully and use gloved hands to rub the seedpods, allowing the seed and chaff to fall onto the sheet. You can also bang the plant against a bowl or other container, allowing the seedpods to shatter on their own and the seeds to fall into the container. The chaff and stems can be composted or stored for tinder for starting campfires or backyard wood fire pits (if allowed in your area). Carefully gather the sheet and pour the seeds and chaff into a large bowl. Flap the sheet to clean off dust, and then, when the wind is blowing, stand over the sheet and pour the seeds and chaff onto the middle of the sheet. Because the chaff is lighter than the seed, the wind will carry the chaff away from the seed, separating the seed from the chaff. The slower you pour the seed, the better the chaff will separate. Once all the seed has been poured out of the bowl, gather

SEEDS IN WHAT YEAR?	Second year
ISOLATION DISTANCE:	One mile
SHATTERING RATE:	Quick
POPULATION MINIMUM:	10+ plants

the sheet and carefully pour the contents back into the bowl. If you are saving seed only for home use, you have now cleaned the seed well enough for home use. If you want the seed to be perfectly clean or if you want to give the seed for gifts, repeat the chaffing process several more times. Because you pulled the entire plants up by the roots to dry, there will likely be some small specks of soil and mud mixed in with the seeds. To get rid of this, wash the seeds by filling the seed bowl with water, swishing the water with your hand, and then slowly pouring the seed into a wire-mesh sieve small enough to capture the seed. Wire mesh sieves are available in the kitchen section of grocery stores and cost only a few dollars. At the bottom of the bowl will be the heaviest material, including dirt and small rocks. Throw these out, even if you have to throw out a few seeds with it. You can repeat this washing process as many times as you want, but all washing should be done at one time and not over several days. Once the seeds are washed, put them on a jelly roll pan or cookie sheet with a lip and shake the seeds gently so they spread flat on the metal sheet. Allow them to air-dry out of direct sunlight until they are completely dry, which can take up to a week. After they are completely dry, the seeds can be stored in a jar or bag.

LEEKS

SEED-CLEANING METHOD

Thresh and winnow. When the seed heads are dry, rub them to release the seeds, or uproot the plant carefully and hit it against the inside of a large box or plastic storage container to release and capture the seeds. Be careful when touching the dried plant in the garden, because movement can cause seeds to fall to the ground. You may want to place an old sheet on the ground under the plant before trying to harvest seeds or uproot the plant.

RECOMMENDED VARIETIES

Belgian breeder's winter mix or American flag, both available at SeedRenaissance.com.

HOW TO SAVE SEEDS

Leeks will go to seed in the second year. Leeks will easily self-seed if you allow the seed to drop to the ground, but the leeks that sprout the next spring will

Leek hats

likely need to be transplanted so they are not too close together. To save leek seeds, allow the globe-shaped seed heads to dry in the garden. Once half of the individual seed capsules have opened to expose the seed, cut the stems and gather the seeds. If you wait longer, the seeds will begin to fall to the ground. Air-dry the seeds indoors for several days to make sure they are completely dry before storage.

SPECIES:	*Allium ampeloprasum*
EASY TO SAVE SEEDS?	Likely yes, if planting one variety per year within one species.
SEED TYPE REQUIRED FOR SEED SAVING:	Heirloom (open-pollinated) seeds (available at SeedRenaissance.com).
NUMBER OF VARIETIES AVAILABLE:	Several
LIFE SPAN OF PLANT:	Annual
LIFE SPAN OF SEED:	Germination decreases after three years of ideal storage. Ideal storage means avoiding drastic temperature fluctuations by keeping seeds in a cool, dark, dry place.
SEED MATURATION:	Allow seeds to dry fully on the plant in the garden or mature as long as possible in garden, pull up the whole plant, roots and all, dry in a cool dark place, like a garage, and then harvest seeds.
FLOWER TYPE:	Perfect
SEX TYPE:	Outbreeding
CROSSES WITH:	All leek varieties and all varieties of elephant garlic. Does not cross with onions.
POLLINATION TYPE:	Insect
SEEDS IN WHAT YEAR?	Second year
ISOLATION DISTANCE:	One mile
SHATTERING RATE:	Slow. Harvest when half of the seed head (globe shaped) is dry and showing seeds. Otherwise, you risk the seeds dropping to the ground in a wind.
POPULATION MINIMUM:	5+ plants

LETTUCE

SEED-CLEANING METHOD

Thresh and winnow. *Caution:* Lettuce plants and flower heads extrude a white latex sap that can be quite sticky. Some lettuce varieties produce more of this sap on the flowers and flower stems than other varieties. Because the sap can be difficult to wash off, you may want to wear disposable gloves if you are gathering more than a few seeds. Also note that many insects seem attracted to this milky, sticky sap. When gathering lettuce seeds, you are likely to find many small insects, and even spiders, among your seeds. Washing the seeds in hot water can help clean them and remove tiny insects. Be sure, however, to quickly spread the wet seeds in a thin layer to air-dry on a cookie sheet, or the damp seeds will sprout overnight. Damp lettuce seeds will produce tiny sprouts within hours, and sprouted seeds are no longer viable for saving.

If I had to choose the easiest vegetable of all to save seed from, lettuce would have to be it. Lettuce is self-fertile, so all you have to do is plant the seed, allow it to grow, don't eat it all, and let a few plants go to seed. Lettuce seed rarely crosses, even if different varieties are grown side by side. Lettuce has never crossed in my garden. However, for the long-term genetic health of the plants, I think it is a good idea to save

SPECIES:	*Lactuca sativa*
EASY TO SAVE SEEDS?	Yes Note: Birds may compete with you for the seeds.
SEED TYPE REQUIRED FOR SEED SAVING:	Heirloom (open-pollinated) seeds (available at SeedRenaissance.com).
NUMBER OF VARIETIES AVAILABLE:	Many
LIFE SPAN OF PLANT:	Annual (can be biennial when protected in winter)
LIFE SPAN OF SEED:	Germination decreases after three years of ideal storage. Ideal storage means avoiding drastic temperature fluctuations by keeping seeds in a cool, dark, dry place.
SEED MATURATION:	Allow seeds to dry fully on the plant in the garden or mature as long as possible in garden, pull up the whole plant, roots and all, dry in a cool dark place, like a garage, and then harvest seeds.
FLOWER TYPE:	Perfect
SEX TYPE:	Inbreeding
CROSSES WITH:	All varieties of lettuce and celtuce, and may cross with some wild lettuces.
POLLINATION TYPE:	Self-pollinating
SEEDS IN WHAT YEAR?	First year
ISOLATION DISTANCE:	None
SHATTERING RATE:	Slow
POPULATION MINIMUM:	3+ plants

seed from several plants a year, instead of a single plant. Saving seeds from just one plant each harvest could potentially create a genetic bottleneck in the future, even though the plants are self-fertile.

RECOMMENDED VARIETIES

Buttercrunch Lettuce
This is my favorite perennial lettuce, as detailed in my *Forgotten Skills* book. In my garden, this lettuce comes back year after year if grown on ground you don't till. It is not a true perennial, but it self-seeds extremely reliably if you don't eat it all and let a few heads go to seed. It has dwarf-sized, green leaves and is one of the first to self-seed in spring, usually in late April or early May. Buttercrunch grows fast and works well for fresh winter garden growing as well as summer. It's a very reliable self-seeder!

Caleb's Deep Winter Lettuce
Winner! All seed of this variety is taken only from plants that spent the winter in in Caleb's backyard garden without any protection, despite temperatures of 19 degrees below zero! Above is a photo of this lettuce in a cold frame in my garden in December. I planted ten federal seed bank accession varieties on October 1 and grew them all winter without any cover or frame—and this variety was the clear winner! I am the only person in the world to offer this seed for sale, and because I developed the seed, I got to name it. It works well for fresh winter garden growing as well as summer growing.

Gabriella Lettuce
This is an amazing deep wine red lettuce that is a must-have for gourmet salads. It's a great tasting, loose-leaf bunching lettuce. This lettuce is dark, dark red from the day it comes out of the ground, and it never changes color. Even better, it was the very last lettuce to bolt in my garden, lasting mid-way through the heat of July. It's a new favorite of mine that works well for fresh winter garden growing as well as summer.

Grand Rapids Lettuce
Winner! This is the all-time fastest growing lettuce in all seasons of the more than 100 varieties of lettuce I have trialed! This stuff grows amazingly fast in fall and in spring, and it even (astonishingly) grew a staggering four inches a week in February in a hotbed! The photo above shows this lettuce in my garden in November—six weeks after being planted from seed, it was a foot tall! This winter lettuce was the winner of an 1899 winter garden lettuce trial by the Extension service. The leaves are delicate and not crunchy, and the flavor is mild. I will never be

Lettuce bolting

Green Oakleaf Lettuce
A frilly green lettuce that is extremely hardy—grows outside in my winter garden without any protection, but grows three times faster in a cold frame. Gorgeous lettuce that is a must-have for gourmet salad mixes, with a fine flavor. The picture on the left was taken in my garden on November 19. The oakleaf is the top two rows of lettuce. It works well for fresh winter garden growing as well as summer growing.

Marvel of Four Seasons Lettuce
This is a favorite of ours because of its stunning color—a red/bronze/green with touches of purple. The lettuce also has a better taste than most lettuces, and best of all, it grows well during all four seasons (cold frame in winter). It works well for fresh winter garden growing as well as growing in the summer, and it's a reliable self-seeder.

North Pole Lettuce
I am the only seller of this lettuce (at SeedRenaissance.com, fifty seeds per pack) in the US. This is a winner of my winter greenhouse lettuce trials. Originally bred a century ago by the famous Norwegian scientist Fridtjof Nansen, who was awarded the Nobel Prize for peace in 1922. He is famous for pioneering exploration of the North Pole and his global work to stop starvation during and after the First World War. For more information about him, see the second chapter of my new *More Forgotten Skills* book. North Pole is a butterhead lettuce.

Tom Thumb Lettuce
This is actually an old French heirloom lettuce that was used for winter growing for hundreds of years. In my 2013 geothermal greenhouse trial of twenty lettuce varieties, this lettuce came in second place, sprouting from seed in the first week of January—you read that right—during a very snowy, bitter cold week when the high temperature in the greenhouse was 34 degrees and the low was 28 degrees. (There is no artificial heat or electricity in my geothermal greenhouse). This lettuce does well outside in cold frames during the winter (down to 7 degrees below zero in my garden), and also grows very well outside in the spring and fall. It has beautiful, round, green, loose leaf heads. This is a dwarf size and is also cut-and-come-again, meaning you can cut it at ground level and it will grow back several times.

Winter Density Lettuce
This is a very old winter lettuce that has been used in winter gardens for hundreds of years. It performs

without this lettuce—If I'm running low on lettuce (we are self-sufficient on lettuce, meaning we grow all we eat) this is the lettuce I plant first. This lettuce came to be in 1880 when Eugene Davis of Grand Rapids, Michigan, noticed that some variants of an ancient French winter lettuce called curled silesia were doing better than all others during winter. Mr. Davis saved seed from the best winter plants until other gardeners began to ask him for the seed. According to an article in the April 1, 1906, edition of *Gardening* magazine, this lettuce "was so well adapted for winter forcing (in cold frames and hotbeds) that it came to be almost exclusively used by Grand Rapids gardeners and growers in other cities came to ask for 'that Grand Rapids lettuce' and seedsmen were obliged to add it to their lists." I love this lettuce and its history. This lettuce is rarely grown today. That will change if I have my way! Works well for fresh winter garden growing as well as summer growing.

Lettuce fluff

to bolt (produce a seed stalk) in summer. In autumn, the stalk will produce flowers. Seeds are ready to be harvested when the flowers die back to produce small white dandelion-like fluffs. Seeds can be collected by carefully knocking the flower head against the inside of a bowl—the seeds will drop into the bowl. The flowers produce seeds over six to eight weeks, so if you are careful, you can knock the seeds off the heads without picking the plants or breaking the stems—this allows you to gather more seeds over time. However, you can also pick the whole plant, let it dry in the garden for several days (or in a shed if weather is going to be rainy), and then collect the seeds. Lettuce seeds are often covered in insects of all kinds, including aphids. Wash them in hot tap water to kill aphids and other insects, then immediately spread the seeds thinly on a cookie sheet to dry near a fan. Seeds that do not dry quickly will sprout, so be careful. Seeds are stored in a container in a cool, dry, dark place once they are completely dry.

excellently in my winter cold frames! This is a green leaf lettuce with a slightly sweet flavor. It works well for fresh winter garden growing as well as summer growing.

Winter Green Jewel Romaine
This is the very best of all winter lettuces, and the lettuce I grow the most on my property year-round. I love the crunch and taste, and I love that you can plant huge amounts of this lettuce very thickly and close together. Best of all, cut this lettuce at the soil level and it grows back again and again! It will stay unprotected in the garden into December, and it does well in winter cold frames. It's both cold hardy and heat resistant! This lettuce is sold by no one else in the world, and it works well for fresh winter garden growing as well as summer.

HOW TO SAVE SEEDS
Plant the seeds outdoors in spring. Up to one-third of the outer leaves of the lettuce may be harvested for eating from plants intended for seed saving. Because lettuce plants do not cross, isolation is not generally practiced. Allow the plants

Seeded lettuce

MUSTARD GREENS

SPECIES:	*Brassica juncea* (includes leafy mustard greens and Indian mustard greens).
EASY TO SAVE SEEDS?	Likely yes, if planting one variety per year within one species. Note: Birds will compete with you for the seeds.
SEED TYPE REQUIRED FOR SEED SAVING:	Heirloom (open-pollinated) seeds (available at SeedRenaissance.com).
NUMBER OF VARIETIES AVAILABLE:	Many
LIFE SPAN OF PLANT:	Annual, perennial, and biennial, depending on the variety. Annuals can be biennial when protected in winter.
LIFE SPAN OF SEED:	Germination decreases after three years of ideal storage. Ideal storage means avoiding drastic temperature fluctuations by keeping seeds in a cool, dark, dry place.
SEED MATURATION:	Allow seeds to dry fully on the plant in the garden or mature as long as possible in garden, pull up the whole plant, roots and all, dry in a cool dark place, like a garage, and then harvest seeds.
FLOWER TYPE:	Perfect
SEX TYPE:	Inbreeding
CROSSES WITH:	All mustard greens varieties, including Indian and leaf mustards, as well wild mustards that grow as weeds commonly in the United States. Mustards greens include Osaka purple mustard greens and others. Does not cross with Chinese mustards.
POLLINATION TYPE:	Self-pollinated and insect-pollinated
SEEDS IN WHAT YEAR?	First year (turnips second year)
ISOLATION DISTANCE:	One-half mile
SHATTERING RATE:	Quick
POPULATION MINIMUM:	10+ plants

SEED-CLEANING METHOD

Thresh and winnow. When the seedpods are dry, rub them to release the seeds, or uproot the plant carefully and hit it against the inside of a large box or plastic storage container to release and capture the seeds. Be careful when touching the dried plant in the garden because the slightest shaking can cause hundreds of seeds to fall to the ground. You may want to place an old sheet on the ground under the plant before trying to harvest seeds or uproot the plant.

HOW TO SAVE SEEDS

Mustard greens are generally short-lived plants, producing edible greens as long as temperatures remain cool and bolting to seed once temperatures warm up. For seed-saving purposes, only one variety can be in flower at a time in the garden. Seeds form as pods, which should be harvested soon after they naturally dry on the plant. The pods will naturally shatter and scatter the seed to the ground after about a week, so harvest the seeds quickly or you will risk losing them. Seeds from mustard greens should be harvested only when the pods have dried. The seeds in green pods are not likely to be fully developed, and if harvested and dried, will have low germination or will fail to germinate. Seeds collected from the garden should be brought indoors to air-dry for a few days before being stored in a container in a cool, dry, dark place.

ONIONS

SPECIES:	Allium cepa
CROSSES WITH:	All flower-producing onion and shallot varieties.
EASY TO SAVE SEEDS?	Likely yes, if planting one variety per year within one species.
SEED TYPE REQUIRED FOR SEED SAVING:	Heirloom (open-pollinated) seeds (available at SeedRenaissance.com).
NUMBER OF VARIETIES AVAILABLE:	Many
LIFE SPAN OF PLANT:	Annual
LIFE SPAN OF SEED:	Germination decreases after six years of ideal storage. Ideal storage means avoiding drastic temperature fluctuations by keeping seeds in a cool, dark, dry place.
SEED MATURATION:	Allow seeds to dry fully on the plant in the garden or mature as long as possible in garden, pull up the whole plant, roots and all, and dry in a cool dark place, like a garage. Then harvest seeds.
FLOWER TYPE:	Perfect
SEX TYPE:	Outbreeding
POLLINATION TYPE:	Insect
SEEDS IN WHAT YEAR?	Second year
ISOLATION DISTANCE:	One mile
SHATTERING RATE:	Slow
POPULATION MINIMUM:	10+ plants

SEED-CLEANING METHOD

Thresh and winnow. When the seedpods are dry, rub them to release the seeds, or uproot the plant carefully and hit it against the inside of a large box or plastic storage container to release and capture the seeds. Be careful when touching the dried plant in the garden, because the slightest shaking can cause hundreds of seeds to fall to the ground. You may want to place an old sheet on the ground under the plant before trying to harvest seeds or uproot the plant.

There are many different types of onions grown by gardeners. Some produce flowers and seed, and some do not. Some are started from seed, and some are propagated by bulbs. Some are propagated by bulbils, and some are propagated by seeds and bulbs.

WHEN TO PLANT

Onion seeds can be planted in late autumn for spring germination, in early spring as soon as the ground can be worked, or anytime in spring while the soil is still cool. Onion seeds will not do well if planted in warm summer weather. Onion seeds are generally planted densely in a small space. When they sprout, they look somewhat like grass, with each seed producing a single green stem that is a thin tube. These sprouts are called "onion threads," and when they are two to three inches tall, they can be gently dislodged from the soil and transplanted. They will likely suffer from transplant shock, especially if the threads have been started indoors or in a greenhouse. However, so long as the ground does not freeze, the threads will often produce plants even if they die back completely after being transplanted. The root will often continue to live and produce new shoots. If the ground freezes, the root will die. Onion threads are spaced about five inches apart and buried only about a half-inch in the ground. Over time, a second stem will emerge, and so on. Growth of onion plants is slow in the beginning.

Onions that are planted from seed are divided into three categories: long-day onions, short-day onions, and day-neutral onions (also called intermediate-day onions). This day length refers to the number of hours of sunlight the plant must have on a summer day in order for it to produce a bulb.

Onion seeds popping

Onion heads

Multiplier onions

LONG-DAY ONIONS: Long-day onions do not produce bulbs until there are fourteen hours of summer sun in a day. They are grown in the north, in zone 6 or lower. A long-day onion planted in a short-day zone will never produce a bulb.

SHORT-DAY ONIONS: Short-day onions begin to form bulbs as soon as there are ten hours of summer sun. They are grown in the south, in garden zones 7 and higher. A short-day onion planted in a long-day zone may go to seed before producing a bulb.

DAY-NEUTRAL ONIONS: Day-neutral onions will form a bulb whether the sunlight is long or short. These onions work best in zones 5 and 6.

Wherever you live, it is important to plant the correct variety of onions for your area. For true seed, allow only one variety of onion to flower at a time. If other varieties in your garden begin to produce flower heads, cut them off to maintain varietal purity.

WHEN TO PLANT

Potato (or Multiplier) Onions

Onions that produce bulbs instead of seeds are called potato onions or multiplier onions. These onions are planted as one seed bulb, and that bulb divides into many bulbs over the summer and fall. In autumn, this clump of bulbs is harvested. The largest onions are kept for replanting. The rest are harvested for eating. Onion bulbs can be planted in autumn or spring. Bulbs smaller than one-and-a-half inches in diameter overwinter best. Larger bulbs may need some protection, like a cold frame or row cover. They may also be overwintered under a layer of straw eight to twelve inches thick. Bulb may also be harvested, dried outdoors for one to two days, and then stored indoors over winter in a cool dark place in a burlap bag or a bag made of some other breathable material. Onions should never be stored in closed containers or plastic, because even a small build up of humidity will cause them to sprout roots and then rot. Potato (multiplier) onions can sometimes produce flower stalks and seeds. This will result in much smaller bulbs, and the bulbs may not store through winter. Because flowering is not a trait you want to encourage in multiplier onions, clip off any flower heads that appear.

Walking or Topset Onions

A few rare varieties of onions produce bulbils. These are called Egyptian walking onions or topset onions. These plants produce onions both at the roots and on top of the plants. The onions at the root will be the largest. The onions on top will be bulbils, and will be the largest in the first year. These topset onions will get smaller and smaller each succeeding year if the root bulbs are not transplanted or disturbed. This type of

Second-year onions

onion can be propagated from either root bulbs or topset bulbs. The bulbils can be harvested in summer or fall, stored indoors over winter, and planted in the spring, or planted directly in the soil in autumn. These onions are perennial and extremely cold-tolerant. The bulbs and bulbils should be planted so that the top third of the bulb is uncovered. These perennial onions are called walking onions because they do, in fact, walk, planting themselves as they go. They "walk" by producing bulbils at the top of the plant on stalks. In late summer or early autumn, these thick green stalks dry up, turn brown, and collapse. The weight of the bulbils tips the collapsed stalks to the ground, and the onions plant themselves by growing roots wherever they touch the ground. The bulbils are used in the kitchen as shallot-type onions and were historically prized because they are perennial and will outlive their owners in most cases. Walking onions may occasionally produce flowers, but these flowers—rare themselves—almost never produce true seed. These flowers can cross with other flowering onions in your garden. To prevent crossing, simply remove any flowers that appear on walking onions.

RECOMMENDED VARIETIES

Egyptian Walking Onions
Sold seasonally at SeedRenaissance.com.

Shallot-Type Multiplier Onions
Sold seasonally at SeedRenaissance.com.

Green Mountain Huge Multiplier Onions
These are by far the largest multiplier onions I've ever grown—some of these are the size of softballs. Five bulbs yielded a staggering fifty-five onions in my garden—and every one of them was larger than any other multiplier I've ever grown. Once you have these onions, you never have to buy them again—they multiply each year. This amazing onion was developed over a decade by the wonderful Kelly Winterton. This is a must-have onion for families looking to be self-sufficient. I sell them as seeds at SeedRenaissance.com. To turn these seeds into bulbs, plant them in early spring in a greenhouse and move them outside as soon as the soil can be worked, or plant the seed outside as soon as the soil can be worked. At the end of summer, after the onions have died back, choose the largest bulbs for multiplying. I plant the bulbs in the fall (late September or early October) and cover them with a cold frame if temperatures are bitter. This method grows the largest onions, but you can also choose your largest bulbs in the fall, harvest them, store over winter, and then plant in spring. Because this is landrace seed, you will get onions that are green, red, yellow, and white. Once you have bulbs to grow out, they will come true to color. Always keep your largest bulbs for

Egyptian walking onions

multiplying the next season. Onion seed generally has a life of one to two years, so plant these seeds within one year.

Yellow Spanish Onions
These are my favorite seed-producing storage onions. The flavor is great, and these onions store for months. They are easy to grow and it's easy to collect seed from them.

Walla Walla Onions
These are a favorite onion for many people when it comes to flavor, but keep in mind that walla wallas are not storage onions and will not store through winter.

HOW TO SAVE SEEDS
Onions that produce seed begin to produce flower stalks about mid-summer.

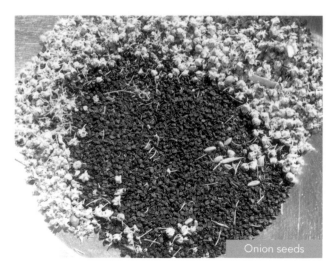
Onion seeds

ORACH

SEED-CLEANING METHOD
Thresh and winnow. A cousin of spinach that is used exactly like spinach, this beautiful red leafy vegetable brings nice color to the winter table and is full of nutrition too. It works well for fresh winter garden growing as well as summer growing.

RECOMMENDED VARIETIES Vernal red orach, available at SeedRenaissance.com.

HOW TO SAVE SEEDS
Allow at least five plants to go to seed. One-third of the leaves may be harvested from the plant without damaging its ability to produce seed. Orach will begin to bolt to seed (produce a seed stalk) in mid-summer. The seeds look like small cereal flakes. Allow the seeds to dry naturally on the plant, and harvest them before they are scattered by the wind. You can harvest the seeds as soon as they begin to change color. Not all seeds dry at the same time, so you will need to harvest several times. For a self-seeding garden, allow some seeds to naturally fall to the ground in a no-till area. Orach will spread if allowed. Pull up any young plants that you don't need. Do not allow orach to spread into the wild or spread out of control. Livestock also love to eat this plant. Seeds should be allowed to completely air-dry indoors, and then can be stored in a container in a cool, dry, dark place.

Orach and cabbage

SPECIES:	*Atriplex hortensis.* Also called mountain spinach, French spinach, sea purslane, and saltbush.
EASY TO SAVE SEEDS?	Likely yes, if planting one variety per year within one species. Note: Birds will compete with you for the seeds.
SEED TYPE REQUIRED FOR SEED SAVING:	Heirloom (open-pollinated) seeds (available at SeedRenaissance.com).
NUMBER OF VARIETIES AVAILABLE:	Several
LIFE SPAN OF PLANT:	Annual
LIFE SPAN OF SEED:	Germination decreases after six years of ideal storage. Ideal storage means avoiding drastic temperature fluctuations by keeping seeds in a cool, dark, dry place.
SEED MATURATION:	Allow seeds to dry fully on the plant in the garden or mature as long as possible in garden, pull up the whole plant, roots and all, and dry in a cool dark place, like a garage. Then harvest seeds.
FLOWER TYPE:	Perfect
SEX TYPE:	Outbreeding
POLLINATION TYPE:	Wind-pollinated
SEEDS IN WHAT YEAR?	First year
ISOLATION DISTANCE:	None
SHATTERING RATE:	Slow
POPULATION MINIMUM:	5+ plants

Orach seeds

PARSNIP

SEED-CLEANING METHOD

Thresh and winnow. When the seedpods are dry, rub them to release the seeds, or uproot the plant carefully and hit it against the inside of a large box or plastic storage container to release and capture the seeds. Be careful when touching the dried plant in the garden because the slightest shaking can cause hundreds of seeds to fall to the ground. You may want to place an old sheet on the ground under the plant before trying to harvest seeds or uproot the plant.

SPECIES:	*Pastinaca sativa*
EASY TO SAVE SEEDS?	Likely yes, if planting one variety per year within one species.
SEED TYPE REQUIRED FOR SEED SAVING:	Heirloom (open-pollinated) seeds (available at SeedRenaissance.com).
LIFE SPAN OF PLANT:	Biennial
LIFE SPAN OF SEED:	Germination decreases after one year of ideal storage. Ideal storage means avoiding drastic temperature fluctuations by keeping seeds in a cool, dark, dry place.
SEED MATURATION:	Allow seeds to dry fully on the plant in the garden or mature as long as possible in garden, pull up the whole plant, roots and all, and dry in a cool dark place, like a garage. Then harvest seeds.
FLOWER TYPE:	Andromonoecious
SEX TYPE:	Outbreeding
CROSSES WITH:	All varieties of parsnip. Does not cross with carrots.
POLLINATION TYPE:	Insect-pollinated
SEEDS IN WHAT YEAR?	Second year
ISOLATION DISTANCE:	One mile
SHATTERING RATE:	Slowly
POPULATION MINIMUM:	10+ plants

Note: Parsnips can be difficult to germinate, especially in dry or hot weather.

There is great news and bad news when it comes to parsnips. The great news is that parsnips don't cross with carrots. Many people have asked me, considering how difficult it is to save pure carrot seed for a backyard gardener, what do we do instead? Parsnips are the answer. They can often be used to replace carrots at the dinner table. And it's much easier to save seed from parsnips. Great news, right? Here's the bad news: parsnip seed has a very short life. Even the freshest seed has low germination rates, so saving parsnip seed really means you have a year or less to get the seed in the ground. The longer you wait, the fewer seeds that will sprout.

RECOMMENDED VARIETIES

All heirloom varieties are worthy of the garden and taste great. Hollow crown and All American are favorites of mine, and both are available at SeedRenaissance.com.

HOW TO SAVE SEEDS

Seeds are produced from second-year plants and should not be saved from first-year plants, as this promotes diminished root development. Plant the seeds in early spring, allow them to mature the whole season, and then cover them in the ground for winter. Uncover in early spring and allow the plants to sprout and bolt to seed. You can also harvest the parsnip roots in fall, trimming the celery-like leaves to leave just one inch remaining, and keep in a cellar or cold room in sand for winter storage. Replant the roots in early spring as soon as the ground can be worked, and allow to sprout and bolt to seed. The advantage of this method is that the roots are protected from voles and other creatures, but the risk is that parsnips may rot or dry out in storage and never sprout again. For this reason, it is important to replant the roots as soon as the soil can be worked in spring. Parsnip seed is large and flat, bearing some resemblance to orach seed.

Parsnips seeding

PEAS

SEED-CLEANING METHOD

Thresh by rubbing the dried pods together in a container to catch the seeds as they fall from the pods.

Most gardeners want to extend their pea harvest to be as early and late as possible. Fresh peas are a treat. In this section I've included a broad selection of different species that are sometimes called peas, even when they are not common garden peas. All of these different species can be grown in the garden without fear of crossing.

RECOMMENDED VARIETIES

Cascadia Peas
This variety of peas withstands several hard frosts and is extra early and truly prolific, with large peas and the largest harvest. They have a traditional garden pea flavor, and grow on large bushy plants. Available at SeedRenaissance.com.

Golden Sweet Snow Peas
These are extra early and can be harvested as snow peas or regular peas. They're not as prolific as Cascadia, but produce a good harvest. The snow peas are a beautiful pale florescent green. Plants can grow to four feet tall or more. Available at SeedRenaissance.com.

Tom Thumb Peas
This variety produces peas a week earlier, at least, than all other pea varieties (and I have tested hundreds of varieties). It does this by making a very small plant, and each plant produces only a handful of peas. These are great for early food, but will not provide a huge harvest. Available at SeedRenaissance.com.

Peas

HOW TO SAVE SEEDS

The biggest difficulty in saving pea seeds comes from a tiny little pest called a pea weevil. If you don't have weevils in your state, saving pea seeds is easy.

Peas are self-pollinating, and to save the seeds all you need to do is let them mature and dry on the plant, then harvest and plant them the next year. The pea weevil lays tiny eggs on the flowers of peas.

SPECIES:	Several are commonly grown in the garden.
	Peas (common garden peas) [*Pisum sativum*] This kind of pea rarely crosses with other varieties of common garden peas within the Pisum sativum species. It does not cross with other species of peas, and it is self-pollinating and occasionally insect-pollinated. Seed saving may be frustrated by weevils. Isolation is not generally practiced.
	Asparagus pea [*Psopholobus tetragonolobus*] The asparagus pea is also called the winged bean, winged pea, and Manila bean. It crosses with all varieties of asparagus pea and does not cross with other species of peas. It's eaten only when immature. No isolation needed. These peas are most often grown for their decorative flowers.
	Cowpea [*Vigna unguiculata*] Cowpeas cross with all varieties of cowpeas. They do not cross with other species of peas. Isolation is generally not practiced.
	Chickpeas [*Cicer arietinum*] Chickpeas are also called garbanzo beans; they cross with all varieties. They do not cross with other species of peas. Isolate different varieties by one-half mile.
	Lentils [*Lens culinaris*] Lentils cross with all varieties of lentils. No isolation needed.
EASY TO SAVE SEEDS?	Yes
SEED TYPE REQUIRED FOR SEED SAVING:	Heirloom (open-pollinated) seeds (available at SeedRenaissance.com).
NUMBER OF VARIETIES AVAILABLE:	Many
LIFE SPAN OF PLANT:	Annual
LIFE SPAN OF SEED:	Germination decreases after three years of ideal storage. Ideal storage means avoiding drastic temperature fluctuations by keeping seeds in a cool, dark, dry place.
SEED MATURATION:	Allow seeds to dry fully on the plant in the garden or mature as long as possible in garden, pull up the whole plant, roots and all, and dry in a cool dark place, like a garage. Then harvest seeds.
FLOWER TYPE:	Perfect
SEX TYPE:	Inbreeding
POLLINATION TYPE:	Self-pollinating
SEEDS IN WHAT YEAR?	First year
SHATTERING RATE:	Slow
POPULATION MINIMUM:	5+ plants

Dried peas

Cascadia peas

My understanding is that the eggs are enveloped in the developing pea, so they end up inside the mature pea. When the pea is dry, the weevil eggs hatch, and the weevil develops inside the pea and eventually eats its way out, leaving a hole in the pea. Some sources believe the weevil burrows into the pea later. Sometimes these holes are covered with a cap, which means the weevil is still inside the hole. Pea weevils will live for months inside of dry peas saved for seeds. Pea weevils have not arrived in every state yet.

You are not likely to know that you have pea weevils until it comes time to get out the peas that you have saved and you discover holes in your peas, or live or dead weevils in the container with your seed peas. Peas that have a weevil hole in them generally do not sprout, because the weevils have eaten critical parts of the seed. If you have pea weevils, you can try to prevent them from infesting a plant by covering the pea plants just before the pea flowers open and leaving them covered. A wooden frame covered in voile fabric can be used, but the weevils (which fly at this stage) must not be able to crawl under the frame, which they will try to do. Peas grown in a winter greenhouse or cold frames on my property have been free of weevils. I have also found that if I immediately put my dried summer peas in the freezer for three days, it seems to kill the weevil before it can hatch out. If you wait too long, however, the seeds will be no good. Even though all pea seeds are self-pollinating, it is still best to save seeds from groups of ten plants or more so that rare natural pollination crosses may occur as Mother Nature intends, to keep the peas genetically healthy. Keep dried peas in a container in a cool, dry, dark place.

PEPPERS

SPECIES:	Two species are commonly grown in the garden.
	Garden peppers [*Capsicum annuum*] Garden peppers include chili peppers. They cross with all varieties of sweet peppers and chili peppers and do not cross with Tobasco or "squash" peppers.
	Tobasco, "squash," and cayenne peppers [*Capsicum frutescens*] These peppers cross with all varieties of Tobasco and so-called "squash" peppers.
	Cayenne Peppers There are many varieties of this pepper in both the *Capsicum annuum* and *Capsicum frutescens* species.
	Note: Sweet peppers allowed to open-pollinate with hot peppers will turn hot in one or more generations.
EASY TO SAVE SEEDS?	Yes
SEED TYPE REQUIRED FOR SEED SAVING:	Heirloom (open-pollinated) seeds (available at SeedRenaissance.com).
NUMBER OF VARIETIES AVAILABLE:	Many
LIFE SPAN OF PLANT:	Annual
LIFE SPAN OF SEED:	Germination decreases after three years of ideal storage. Ideal storage means avoiding drastic temperature fluctuations by keeping seeds in a cool, dark, dry place.
SEED MATURATION:	Scrape seeds from inside the fruit when the fruit is mature and begins to turn soft. Dry the seeds before storage.
FLOWER TYPE:	Perfect
SEX TYPE:	Inbreeding
POLLINATION TYPE:	Self-pollinated
SEEDS IN WHAT YEAR?	First year
ISOLATION DISTANCE:	Experts recommend fifty feet, but isolation is often not practiced.
SHATTERING RATE:	Not applicable
POPULATION MINIMUM:	5+ plants

SEED-CLEANING METHOD

Scrape from the fruit, wash, and air-dry indoors before storage. Seeds should never be dried in a machine or oven.

RECOMMENDED VARIETIES

Seeds for medicinal cayenne are available at SeedRenaissance .com. There are hundreds of varieties of peppers, and aficionados have strong preferences in garden chili and sweet pepper varieties. Some varieties should be harvested with care, because even touching the skin of the pepper can transfer the oil from the pepper onto the gardener's hands, which can then be transferred to the eyes or to children, causing pain.

HOW TO SAVE SEEDS

The fruit of chili and sweet peppers can be disfigured by natural causes. To discourage this kind of disfiguration in future generations, many gardeners recommend saving seeds only from the most perfect examples of the fruit. Allow the peppers to either go soft or dry in the garden, then harvest the peppers, scrape out the seeds, wash them in warm water, and let them air-dry for several days until completely dry. Store in a container in a cool, dry, dark place.

POTATOES

SPECIES:	*Solanum tuberosum*
EASY TO SAVE SEEDS?	No
SEED TYPE REQUIRED FOR SEED SAVING:	Propagated by saving potatoes. Some potato varieties produce seeds, called TPS (True Potato Seed). TPS is used experimentally to create new lines of potatoes (which are then propagated by saving tubers, which is genetic cloning.)
VARIETIES AVAILABLE:	Many
SEED MATURATION:	To harvest TPS, take the berry formed by the potato flower late in autumn. Scrape the seeds from the berry and allow to dry before storing.
FLOWER TYPE:	Perfect
SEX TYPE:	Inbreeding
CROSSES WITH:	All other flower-producing potatoes. In addition, potatoes are genetic tetraploids, meaning each flower crossing produces sixteen alleles instead of the common four. Note: Finding varieties of potatoes that reliably produce flowers and seeds can be difficult.
POLLINATION TYPE:	Self-pollinated and insect-pollinated
SEEDS IN WHAT YEAR?	First year
ISOLATION DISTANCE:	None
SHATTERING RATE:	Does not shatter
POPULATION MINIMUM:	Not applicable

SEED-CLEANING METHOD

Scrape from the berry, wash, and air-dry indoors before storing.

RECOMMENDED VARIETIES

Mountain Rose is my all-time favorite variety of potato.

Note: Ants tunnel into both potatoes and sweet potatoes, and these roots with holes in them will quickly rot while left outside to cure. Instead of curing them, eat them immediately after harvest. Tubers with holes should not be used for storage because they will rot.

HOW TO SAVE SEEDS

Tuber Method
Potatoes are typically planted using seed potatoes and not seeds from the potato flowers. In fact, most potatoes don't produce flowers anymore, and even when they do, the flowers only rarely produce the berries that contain the seeds. To save some potatoes for planting the next year, do not wash them. Washing potatoes strips away the delicate water-soluble natural enzymes that protect the potatoes from rot. Store them indoors in a cool, dry, dark place. Absolutely darkness is important because even a little light and warmth will encourage the potato to sprout. Potatoes that sprout too early to be planted outside will either rot or desiccate.

Only the best potatoes should be saved as seed potatoes—potatoes that are not bruised or cut. Some gardeners believe that only the largest potatoes should be saved as seed potatoes, but this is a myth. Potatoes are genetic clones and their growth size is dependent on growing conditions and traits of the specific potato variety, rather than saving the largest potatoes. However, some gardeners will dispute me on this, and if you want to save the largest, that is not a problem. Keep in mind, however, that commercial seed potatoes are never the largest—indeed they are often smaller than the "ideal" size for the potato variety. Plant the potatoes the next year. Keep in mind that seed potatoes carry viruses. Commercially certified seed potatoes are grown in special circumstances to guarantee they are virus free, which is something no one who grows them in garden soil can guarantee. Seed potatoes saved from the backyard may fail after several generations when they are overcome by potato viruses or nematodes.

However, many gardeners save their own seed potatoes, at least for a few years. Every few years, new certified virus-free seed potatoes may be needed. You can attempt to grow your own virus-free seed potatoes by sprouting a seed potato over a cup of distilled water. This is generally done by sticking toothpicks in a potato so the potato can be set on top of a glass of water with just the bottom of the potato is touching the water. There should be air space around most of the potato, and the potato should not touch the glass. Leave this in a sunny window, and the potato will sprout. When the sprouts are six to eight inches long, cut off the top four inches and plant them in a sterile potting soil mix. The sprouts you cut off should never have touched the potato. Any part of the sprout that touched the water should also not be used. You want four inches of a sprout that has only ever touched air. Plant the sprout two inches deep in the potting soil and keep it moist. The seedling should not be transplanted outside to the garden until roots have been established. This method may not be foolproof, and no one should touch the sprouts as they grow. However, this method gives gardeners a much better chance of getting disease-free potatoes.

TPS (True Potato Seed) Method

TPS is a growing hobby among potato lovers, because it can provide years of experimentation and exciting results. Some heirloom potatoes will still produce flowers, and those flowers will produce berries that contain seeds. Harvest the berries when they turn slightly soft. They will fall off the potato plant about sixty days after they form, so keep an eye on them if you don't want to lose them. The seeds are scraped from the berries, air-dried, and saved for the next year. Potato seeds are very unusual in the garden, because they are tetraploid, meaning they have four chromosomes instead of the more typical two. Every single seed will produce a potato with different traits. This means that every seed is absolutely unpredictable—and that is what makes working with TPS fun. You are literally inventing new breeds of potatoes. Some may be great, and you will want to save potatoes from them to continue the new line. Others will be worthless (tiny) or intermediate. Diving deep into TPS gardening can be fun. If you want to do more than experiment with TPS, I suggest reading *The Lost Art of Potato Breeding* by Rebsie Fairholm. You can also find some introductory material on her blog at http://daughterofthesoil.blogspot.com.

TPS can be planted directly in the garden, but it does much better when started indoors first. The seedlings can be surprisingly delicate, but they should be transplanted outdoors quickly after sprouting to avoid becoming leggy and weak. TPS seedlings should be protected from harsh weather by a cold frame, if needed. Keep them constantly moist until they are established. TPS likes humidity. TPS is not sold commercially, but look for potato growing forums, where growers are often happy to share their TPS—as well as expert advice and photos of their own potato breeding efforts—with beginners.

RADISHES

SEED-CLEANING METHOD

Thresh and winnow. Note that pods can be successfully planted without threshing. If you wish to separate the seeds from the pods, carefully crush the pods to break them open, and then scrape the dried seeds out of the pod. This process can be labor intensive and is not necessary.

RECOMMENDED VARIETIES

Watermelon radish

This is a variety of radish that is a little sweeter than most radishes and has a green/white outer color and a red inner color resembling a watermelon. Available at SeedRenaissance.com.

Cincinnati market radish

This is a carrot-type radish that is easy to grow and produces radishes shaped like carrots, which are great for roasting. Available at SeedRenaissance.com.

HOW TO SAVE SEEDS

Radish plants will bolt to seed in the heat of summer, producing huge bush-like plants. You should let only one species be in flower at time, or else they will cross. The flowers form seedpods that are the size of

Cincinnati market radish

SPECIES:	*Rhaphanus sativus*
EASY TO SAVE SEEDS?	Likely yes, if planting one variety per year within one species.
SEED TYPE REQUIRED FOR SEED SAVING:	Heirloom (open-pollinated) seeds (available at SeedRenaissance.com).
LIFE SPAN OF PLANT:	Annual
LIFE SPAN OF SEED:	Germination decreases after five years of ideal storage. Ideal storage means avoiding drastic temperature fluctuations by keeping seeds in a cool, dark, dry place.
SEED MATURATION:	Allow seeds to dry fully on the plant in the garden or mature as long as possible in garden, pull up the whole plant, roots and all, and dry in a cool dark place, like a garage. Then harvest seeds.
FLOWER TYPE:	Perfect
SEX TYPE:	Outbreeding
CROSSES WITH:	All varieties of radishes, including wild radishes, which commonly grow as weeds in the United States.
POLLINATION TYPE:	Insect-pollinated
SEEDS IN WHAT YEAR?	First year
ISOLATION DISTANCE:	One-half mile
SHATTERING RATE:	Hard pod
POPULATION MINIMUM:	10+ plants

a pinky finger and pointed at the outer end. These pods should be allowed to dry on the plant. Each pod contains only a few seeds, sometimes as few as two seeds per pod and often three or four seeds per pod. The great news is that these pods can be planted whole. Harvesting seed from these pods can be hard, tedious work made especially frustrating because there are so few seeds in each pod, but once you realize that the seeds actually germinate better when they are left in the pod, you are released from the work of having to thresh the seeds. Collect the pods and allow them to completely dry indoors before storing in a container in a cool, dry, dark place.

Radish flower

RUTABAGA

SEED-CLEANING METHOD

Thresh and winnow. When the seedpods are dry, rub them to release the seeds, or uproot the plant carefully and hit it against the inside of a large box or plastic storage container to release and capture the seeds. Be careful when touching the dried plant in the garden, because the slightest shaking can cause hundreds of seeds to fall to the ground. You may want to place an old sheet on the ground under the plant before trying to harvest seeds or uproot the plant.

RECOMMENDED VARIETIES

Any heirloom variety. Seeds are available at SeedRenaissance.com.

HOW TO SAVE SEEDS

Rutabaga seeds are harvested from second-year bulbs. Learning to harvest rutabaga seeds begins with a caution: some rutabagas might try to bolt (produce seed stalks) in the first year, especially if they are exposed to drought conditions. Do not harvest seed from first-year bulbs. Why? Over the centuries, rutabagas have been "trained" by farmers to form a bulb for harvesting. Their natural inclination is to form seeds instead of a bulb. If you harvest seed from first-year plants, within a few generations of seed, you will have rutabagas that produce only seeds and not root bulbs for eating. The roots will be skinny and useless—and then you have defeated the purpose of having the seed. To correctly produce rutabaga seed, follow these steps:

Step 1

Plant rutabaga seeds and allow them to mature through the summer. Rutabagas prefer a long cool period to get the best bulbs. Where I live, they can only be planted in late summer for an early winter harvest.

Step 2

Carefully harvest the mature rutabaga and select the best and most perfect specimens for seed saving. *Caution:* you can only save

SPECIES:	*Brassica napus*
	Note: Also called Swedes or Swede turnips. Birds may compete with you for the seeds.
EASY TO SAVE SEEDS?	Likely yes, if planting one variety per year within one species.
SEED TYPE REQUIRED FOR SEED SAVING:	Heirloom (open-pollinated) seeds (available at SeedRenaissance.com).
NUMBER OF VARIETIES AVAILABLE:	Several
LIFE SPAN OF PLANT:	Biennial
LIFE SPAN OF SEED:	Germination decreases after five years of ideal storage. Ideal storage means avoiding drastic temperature fluctuations by keeping seeds in a cool, dark, dry place.
SEED MATURATION:	Allow seeds to dry fully on the plant in the garden or mature as long as possible in garden, pull up the whole plant, roots and all, and dry in a cool dark place, like a garage. Then harvest seeds.
FLOWER TYPE:	Perfect
SEX TYPE:	Inbreeding
CROSSES WITH:	All varieties of rutabaga, as well as all varieties of Siberian kale, Hanover salad, and oilseed rape (sometimes just called rape or rapa). Rutabaga may also cross with fodder turnips.
POLLINATION TYPE:	Self-pollinated and insect-pollinated.
SEEDS IN WHAT YEAR?	Second year
ISOLATION DISTANCE:	One mile
SHATTERING RATE:	Quick
POPULATION MINIMUM:	10+ plants

seed from one variety of rutabaga. If you save two or more varieties, they will cross when in flower, which means your seed will be unstable. Unstable seed may produce seed like either parent or like a combination of the two. Unstable seed may not continue to produce good bulbs after several generations, and you will not be able to predict the traits—color, flavor, or size—of the rutabagas produced. For these reasons, be sure that you save bulbs from only one heirloom rutabaga variety per year. The good news is that with ten seed plants, you will produce more than enough seed for several years of gardening, so you will be able to select a new variety for seed saving the next year.

Step 3

Cut the leaves off the rutabagas you have selected for seed saving. You may leave up to an inch of stem. *Caution:* do not cut the bulb of the bulb itself. Even a small cut or scar may cause the rutabaga to spoil in storage. Store these bulbs through winter in damp sand, sawdust, or pine shavings in a cool dark place such as a garage, basement cold room, or cellar. The temperature in your storage space must be cool, but it cannot go below freezing or the rutabagas will likely spoil.

The bulbs will slowly produce leaves in the dark. Pick these leaves off monthly, since they take energy away from the bulb. These leaves are edible and tasty. *Caution:* if you are also preserving rutabagas for eating, make sure you don't mix up the rutabagas you are keeping for eating with the rutabagas you are keeping for seed, or you might eat your future seed-producing bulbs. This might seem like a unlikely scenario, but if you are in the middle of making soup or roasted vegetables in December and you ask a child or spouse to "grab" a rutabaga out of storage for you, and they bring the bulbs you have selected for seed-saving without you realizing it, you have lost your potential for a seed crop. This has happened to me many times!

Step 4

In the spring of the second year, plant the saved bulbs in the outside garden when the ground can be worked. Over the next few weeks the bulbs will begin to produce leaves. The bulbs will bolt (begin to form seed stalks) in early summer. The seeds are mature when the plants begin to dry up and die. *Caution:*

rutabaga seeds are excellent at planting themselves. When dry, the seeds are scattered by wind, rain, and birds. Once they are scattered, they are difficult to retrieve and may spoil if you try to save them, because they are damp or muddy. To harvest the seed, lay a cloth or tarp on the ground under the plant. Wearing a leather glove, put your hand at the base of each beet stem and pull upward, knocking the seeds off the stem onto the tarp.

Step 5

Once you have harvested the seeds, allow them to air-dry outside for several hours, up to a full day. This allows any bugs time to leave the seeds before you bring them indoors. However, while you are airing out your seeds outdoors, make sure they will not be exposed to water, wind, or birds.

Step 6

Bring the seeds indoors for several days to dry. Air-drying should be done indoors to avoid weather, moisture, wind, and birds. Once seeds are completely dry, they can be stored in a paper, glass, or plastic container.

Alternative option

Instead of harvesting bulbs in the fall, storing them for winter, and replanting them in spring, there is a method for leaving them in the garden over winter. In late fall, before the ground freezes, cover the bulbs with twelve inches of loose straw, hay, or pine needles. Do not cover with a layer of leaves, because leaves can smother the roots by forming a mat that does not allow airflow. Snow cover is good and helps create a "blanket" over the straw layer. The covering is important to keep the ground around the bulbs from freezing, which will kill the bulbs. In early spring, as soon as the ground thaws, uncover the bulbs and allow them to grow and go to seed as described above. *Caution:* rodents may eat the bulbs left in the garden to overwinter. Severe weather may freeze and kill the bulbs.

SOYBEANS

SPECIES:	Glycine max
EASY TO SAVE SEEDS?	Likely yes, if planting one variety per year within one species.
SEED TYPE REQUIRED FOR SEED SAVING:	Heirloom (open-pollinated) seeds (available at SeedRenaissance.com).
NUMBER OF VARIETIES AVAILABLE:	Several
LIFE SPAN OF PLANT:	Annual
LIFE SPAN OF SEED:	Germination decreases after three years of ideal storage. Ideal storage means avoiding drastic temperature fluctuations by keeping seeds in a cool, dark, dry place.
SEED MATURATION:	Allow seeds to dry fully on the plant in the garden or mature as long as possible in garden, pull up the whole plant, roots and all, and dry in a cool dark place, like a garage. Then harvest seeds.
FLOWER TYPE:	Perfect
SEX TYPE:	Inbreeding
CROSSES WITH:	Rarely crosses with other varieties of soybeans.
POLLINATION TYPE:	Self-pollinated. Isolation is not generally practiced.
SEEDS IN WHAT YEAR?	First year
ISOLATION DISTANCE:	None
SHATTERING RATE:	Quick
POPULATION MINIMUM:	5+ plants

SEED-CLEANING METHOD

Thresh by rubbing the dried pods together in a container to catch the seeds as they fall from the pods.

HOW TO SAVE SEEDS

Allow the mature beans to dry on the vine. As they begin to dry, you will need to pay attention, because soybean pods break themselves open when dry by forming corkscrew curls. The seeds will then drop to the ground and can become lost. They are best harvested in the small window after the pods dry but before they corkscrew. If the beans do fall, they can be gathered if they don't get wet or muddy. In my garden, the beans drop to the ground each year and are self-planting, meaning I never have to plant edamame because they plant themselves each year. If you collect the seeds, store them in a container in a cool, dry, dark place. Edamame is simply a Japanese word that has been adopted for varieties of soybeans that are eaten as shelly beans, meaning the green beans are removed from the pod and eaten fresh and raw as a snack or side dish. Soybeans are an excellent source of protein and nutrition.

Soybeans

SPINACH

SEED-CLEANING METHOD

Thresh and winnow. When the seed clusters are dry, strip them from the stem by pulling along the stem with a gloved hand. Prepare a box, bowl, or sheet for the seeds to fall into. Be careful when touching the dried plant in the garden, because movement can cause seeds to fall to the ground.

RECOMMENDED VARIETIES

America spinach is the best because it is prolific, easy to grow, and has the best cold soil and winter tolerance. America spinach loves cold weather!

HOW TO SAVE SEEDS

Spinach plants are either entirely male or entirely female. For best results, you will need at least

Spinach seeder

twenty plants for healthy genetics and strong seed. Only the female plants will produce seeds. Spinach planted in spring may go to seed in autumn if your growing season is long enough. Autumn-planted spinach will also go to seed in the second year if you cover the plants over winter with a cold frame, cloche, row cover, or other protection. One-third of the leaves can be harvested from the plants in the first year without affecting the plant's ability to produce seeds. The plants will die if the ground freezes. Allow the plants to mature and bolt (form a seed stalk). Harvest the seeds after they naturally dry on the stalk. Spinach seeds usually dry before the stalk dries and quickly fall to the earth, so it is important to keep an eye on the plants and harvest the seeds as soon as they are dry. The easiest way to harvest the seeds is to strip them from the stock using a leather-gloved hand. Put a large bowl or cloth under the plant to capture the seed as you strip it from the stalk. Store the seeds in a container in a cool, dry, dark place.

SPECIES:	*Spinacia oleracea*
EASY TO SAVE SEEDS?	Likely yes, if planting one variety per year within one species.
SEED TYPE REQUIRED FOR SEED SAVING:	Heirloom (open-pollinated) seeds (available at SeedRenaissance.com).
NUMBER OF VARIETIES AVAILABLE:	Many
LIFE SPAN OF PLANT:	Annual (can be biennial when protected in winter)
LIFE SPAN OF SEED:	Germination decreases after five years of ideal storage. Ideal storage means avoiding drastic temperature fluctuations by keeping seeds in a cool, dark, dry place.
SEED MATURATION:	Allow seeds to dry fully on the plant in the garden or mature as long as possible in garden, pull up the whole plant, roots and all, and dry in a cool dark place, like a garage. Then harvest seeds.
FLOWER TYPE:	Dioecious
SEX TYPE:	Outbreeding
CROSSES WITH:	All varieties of spinach. Does not cross with wild spinach (Lamb's Quarters) or orach. Note: Birds will compete with you for the seeds.
POLLINATION TYPE:	Wind
SEEDS IN WHAT YEAR?	First year
ISOLATION DISTANCE:	Five miles
SHATTERING RATE:	Quick
POPULATION MINIMUM:	20+ plants

Spinach seeds

SQUASH AND PUMPKINS

SPECIES:	Four main species are used in most gardens.

Cucurbita maxima
This crosses with all banana squash varieties, buttercup squash varieties, Hubbard squash varieties, turban squash varieties, and marrow squash varieties, as well as Amish pie, Australian pumpkin, and others.

Cucurbita mixta
Cucurbita mixta crosses with most varieties of cushaw squash, all varieties of wild seroria squash, and silver-seeded gourds, as well as big white crookneck, Cochita Pueblo squash, and others. Does not cross with golden cushaw, orange cushaw, or orange-striped cushaw.

Cucurbita moschata
This plant crosses with all varieties of butternut squash and cheese squash, golden cushaw, orange cushaw, orange-striped cushaw, sweet potato squash, citrouille d'Eysines, field pumpkins, and Futtsu, Kikuza, Landreth, Long Island, Tennessee, and Napoli squash. It also crosses with rampicante (also called tromboncino) and others.

Cucurbita pepo
Pepo crosses with all varieties of summer squash, as well as acorn, cocozelle, crookneck, scallop, zucchini, and vegetable marrow squash, and most gourds. It also crosses with Connecticut field pumpkin and delicata, early prolific straightneck, fordhook, and scallopini squash, as well as Jack-O'-Lantern pumpkins, Howden squash, Japanese pie, Lakota, naked seeded squash, New England pie, Patisson squash, potimarron, Rocky Mountain pie, Rondo de Nice, straightneck, small sugar squash, Thelma Sanders, spaghetti squash (also called vegetable spaghetti), winter pie, and Xochitlan Pueblo, among others.

SEED-CLEANING METHOD
Scrape seeds from the squash. Wash and air-dry indoors before storage. Seeds should never be dried in a machine or oven.

HOW TO SAVE SEEDS
Isolation by Species
In my *More Forgotten Skills* book I called this method "The Magic Four" because you can choose one squash variety from each of the four squash species described in this chapter to plant in your garden. The squash will not cross-pollinate between species, so you can grow one of each species in the same garden without concern. However, keep in mind that squash can be pollinated by any variety of the same species within a half-mile radius of your garden, and you cannot control the insects or what the neighbors are growing. This means that if your neighbor a block away grows Costata zucchini and you grow dark green zucchini, insects are highly likely to cross the two. The likelihood of a natural cross is even greater the closer the neighboring gardens are together.

If you live surrounded by many homes, isolation by species may not work for you. If a natural cross occurs, there will be no physical evidence until the seed is planted, grown out, and producing the next generation of squash. This next generation will produce unstable squash, meaning they will be different colors, shapes, sizes, and flavors. The seed from these plants will never be stable again without years of isolation work—and even then the only thing you could hope to create is a new squash variety. It would be very difficult to get contaminated squash seed to return to the varietal purity of its parents. For practical purposes, the isolation by species method is usually not used in suburban areas.

EASY TO SAVE SEEDS?	This depends on whether your neighbors are gardening. If people near you have squash in bloom, insects are highly likely to cross them. If your own garden, you can plant one variety per year within one species and hope for the best, or you can practice hand-pollination to control purity and prevent promiscuous crossing.
SEED TYPE REQUIRED FOR SEED SAVING:	Heirloom (open-pollinated) seeds (available at SeedRenaissance.com). Caution: A surprising number of summer squash seeds are now genetically modified.
NUMBER OF VARIETIES AVAILABLE:	Many
LIFE SPAN OF PLANT:	Annual
LIFE SPAN OF SEED:	Germination decreases after six years of ideal storage. Ideal storage means avoiding drastic temperature fluctuations by keeping seeds in a cool, dark, dry place.
FLOWER TYPE:	Monoecious
SEX TYPE:	Outbreeding
POLLINATION TYPE:	Insect
SEEDS IN WHAT YEAR?	First year
ISOLATION DISTANCE:	One-half mile
SHATTERING RATE:	Does not shatter
POPULATION MINIMUM:	4+ plants if hand-pollinating or more for open pollination

Isolation by Distance

For practical purposes, this method is usually not used. To isolate varieties by distance, you must be able to ensure that no varieties in the same species are flowering within a half-mile radius. Most backyard gardeners do not control enough property to make this practical.

Hand-Pollination of Squash

This is the method most used by home gardeners.

Step 1

Identify which squash flowers are approaching sexual maturity. The first flowers on a squash plant produce the most vigorous seeds, so watch as flowers begin to form. Using immature flowers will fail to produce viable seed. Squash flowers begin to turn yellow at the tips the evening before they open, and this is how you can identify which flowers to work with.

Step 2

Identify which flowers are male and which are female. Squash flowers are either male or female. Male flowers have only a stem topped by a flower. Female flowers have a stem topped by an immature fruit, which is topped by a flower. For best results, you will need three male flowers, each from a different squash plant, to pollinate one female flower. This means working with four flowers for every squash you hope to save. All plants must be from the same variety of squash. If not, you will not have true seed and the resulting fruit will be an unpredictable, unstable genetic mix that will produce different colors, flavors, and sizes of squash each generation.

Step 3

In the evening, after identifying the flowers that are preparing to open the next day, use tape to seal the flowers so they cannot open the next morning. Or use one pollination bag on each flower. Pollination bags are made of fabric, have drawstrings, and are reusable and washable. Sets are available at SeedRenaissance.com. Any flower that opens on its own will not be usable for seed saving, because it will have been promiscuously pollinated by insects and will not produce true seed.

Step 4

The next morning, snip the three sealed or bagged male flowers from the their plants. Carefully remove the petals entirely to expose the pollen-covered anther inside. Be careful not to smudge or disturb the pollen on the anther. Set these aside for a moment on something that will keep them clean and will not disturb the pollen. The anther

Female squash

will be naturally coated in dusty yellow pollen.

Step 5
Cut, pinch, or tear just the tip off the female flower. The flower will slowly begin to open, revealing the yellow stigma of the female flower.

Step 6
Like an artist holding a painting brush, one at a time, use the male flower anthers to gently "paint" pollen onto the female stigma. The pollen from each male flower should be pressed all around the stigma without damaging the stigma.

Step 7
Use tape or the pollination bag to close and seal the female flower petals. If using tape, cover the entire flower. Insects must not be able to gain access to the stigma, so make sure the flower is tightly protected, but be certain not to damage the flower or stem or the

flower will die. Insects will attempt to chew through the flower petals to get to the pollen they can smell inside, or they will try to wedge their way beneath the pollination bag if it is not tied securely enough. The insects will bring random squash pollen to the flower, and then the flower will not produce true seed. On the other hand, if you are not careful when you seal the flower with tape or a bag, you will bruise or break the flower, and it will die without producing a squash.

Step 8
Mark the stem. I loosely tie a red piece of yarn to the stem.

Step 9
Leave the flower bagged or taped closed for two to three days. If you are using tape, the flower will naturally die back and fall off. If you are using a bag, remove the bag after the flower has fully wilted and died back inside, which takes two to three days. Remove the bag so the immature squash is not damaged.

Step 10
If your hand-pollination was successful, a squash will begin to grow on that stem. Make sure the stem remains clearly marked so that you can find the squash among the others at the end of the season.

Step 11
At the end of the growing season, once the whole squash plant has died back, remove the squash from the garden. Mark it so that you will be able to tell it from the other squash you may harvest for later eating.

Step 12
Store the squash in a cool, dry, dark place until Christmas. Squash are slow and particular seed producers, and if the squash is not stored long enough, the seed will not fully develop inside. To be safe, store them until Christmas. Around Christmas, cut the squash open, scrape out the seeds and fiber, and separate the seeds from the squash fiber. Wash the seeds. Arrange them in a single layer on a cookie sheet or platter lined with wax paper, parchment, or a silicone baking liner. Allow them to air dry for at least a week until they are completely dry and not cool to the touch. Do not use any heat source to dry the seeds. Once the seeds are completely dry, you can store them in a closed container until you are ready to plant them the next summer.

Step 13

Grow the seeds out to test them. This is an important step because you will not know for sure whether you kept the flower sealed from insects until you grow out the seed and physically see that it produces squash that are true to the parents.

Trouble Shooting Failed Hand-Pollination

If your hand-pollination was not successful, the stem and immature squash will wither on the vine and die. This will happen within forty-eight hours of your hand-pollination attempt. Here are some possible reasons why hand-pollination fails:

- Either the male or female flowers were not sexually mature. It takes a little experience and observation before you can truly tell which flowers are going to open the next day. Using a flower that is one day too immature is not likely to produce a squash.

- The anther or stigma of the flowers was damaged when handled.

Pumpkin seeds

Squash with dead blossom

- The pollen was not pressed firmly enough to transfer from the male flowers to the female flower.

- The female flower head was cracked, bruised, or damaged in the process of pollination. This is the most likely cause of pollination failure.

- Finally, there is a high natural rate of spontaneous abortion among squash flowers that is not fully understood by science. Even if you have done everything perfectly, there is a real chance that the pollinated flower will die. This happens to as many as a third of all natural squash pollinations in the garden, so don't take it personally. Any gardener who has practiced the art of hand-pollinating squash has experienced failure. The good news is that you will know within forty-eight hours whether the squash is going to develop, and if it doesn't you'll have time to try again.

SUNCHOKES (JERUSALEM ARTICHOKES)

SPECIES:	*Helianthus tuberosus* Note: Sunchokes produce flowers and seeds, but the seeds are usually naturally sterile. Seeds are not used for propagation. Instead, the plants are propagated by tuber cuttings or shoots, which are called "slips."
EASY TO SAVE SEEDS?	Yes. Tubers readily self-perpetuate.
LIFE SPAN OF PLANT:	Perennial. Potentially invasive if given regular access to water.
SEED MATURATION:	Tubers are harvested each spring. They can be planted in spring or autumn.
CROSSES WITH:	Nothing. Also called Jerusalem Artichoke and sunroot.
SEEDS IN WHAT YEAR?	Tubers produced each year.

This vegetable is kind of like a cross between a potato and a sunflower, believe it or not. The tuber roots are eaten in soups and stews and are prized because they are not starchy and are low on the glycemic scale. These roots are also prized because they are ready to harvest in February, making them an important "hunger gap" food for previous generations for whom self-reliance was a necessity. The plants grow to eight feet tall and, in mid-autumn, bloom with yellow sunflowers that are about a third smaller than common wild sunflowers (sunchokes do not cross with garden or wild sunflowers). I should also mention that sunchokes have historically been called Jerusalem artichokes, but because they have nothing to do with Jerusalem and they are not at all related to artichokes, there has been a movement among gardeners to change the name to sunchokes to better reflect the nature of this vegetable.

RECOMMENDED VARIETIES There are no varieties.

HOW TO SAVE SEEDS

No effort is necessary. Simply do not harvest all of the tubers. Leave some in the ground, and they will grow more tubers. No storage is necessary—tubers can stay in the ground in almost any climate year-round. They are very hardy.

SUNFLOWERS

SEED-CLEANING METHOD

Thresh. Shells do not need to be removed from seeds before planting. Allow the seed head to dry completely before harvesting. Cover the drying head with mesh if necessary to protect the seeds from birds. Using a gloved hand, rub the seeds to loosen them from the seed head.

RECOMMENDED VARIETIES

Any heirloom variety.

HOW TO SAVE SEEDS

If you have wild sunflowers growing in your area, saving seeds from your garden sunflowers should be considered an experiment, because they may cross. However, many gardeners successfully save sunflower seeds. Be aware, however, that the fact that the first generation of your seeds seems pure and true when grown out does not guarantee true seeds. Remember that crossed (unstable) genetics drift over time, with the wild traits (usually smaller flowers) manifesting more prominently after several generations.

Plant your seeds and allow the plants to mature. Allow the seed heads to dry completely in the garden. You may need to cover them with a fine mesh to keep birds from stealing them as they dry. Once the heads are dry, bring them indoors to dry further, out of direct sunlight. To remove the seeds from the head, rub the head with your hands while wearing gloves. Rubbing will eventually loosen some of the seeds, and once some of the seeds have begun to fall out, it will be easier to loosen the others. Store the seeds in a cool, dark, dry place, in a container, until ready to use. Seeds do not need to be hulled to be planted.

SPECIES:	*Helianthus annuus*
EASY TO SAVE SEEDS?	Likely yes, if planting one variety per year within one species. Some gardeners say that, in their experience, sunflowers don't cross easily. But remember, as discussed earlier in this book, crossed phenotypes often take several years to manifest within a breed line. Note: Birds will compete with you for the seeds.
SEED TYPE REQUIRED FOR SEED SAVING:	Heirloom (open-pollinated) seeds (available at SeedRenaissance.com).
NUMBER OF VARIETIES AVAILABLE:	Many
LIFE SPAN OF PLANT:	Annual
LIFE SPAN OF SEED:	Germination decreases after seven years of ideal storage. Ideal storage means avoiding drastic temperature fluctuations by keeping seeds in a cool, dark, dry place.
SEED MATURATION:	Allow seeds to dry fully on the plant in the garden or mature as long as possible in garden, pull up the whole plant, roots and all, and dry in a cool dark place, like a garage. Then harvest seeds.
FLOWER TYPE:	Perfect
SEX TYPE:	Outbreeding
CROSSES WITH:	All varieties of garden sunflowers and some wild sunflowers.
POLLINATION TYPE:	Insect
SEEDS IN WHAT YEAR?	First year
ISOLATION DISTANCE:	One-half mile
SHATTERING RATE:	Quick
POPULATION MINIMUM:	10+ plants

SWEET POTATOES

SPECIES:	*Ipomoea batatas*
SEED TYPE REQUIRED FOR SEED SAVING:	Sweet potatoes do not produce seeds. Instead, they are propagated by tuber cutting or shoots, which are called "slips."
NUMBER OF VARIETIES AVAILABLE:	Many

SEED-CLEANING METHOD

You can store sweet potatoes over winter in damp sand or pine shavings. Slips are grown in late spring and planted after all danger of frost is past

BUYING SLIPS

I recommend ordering slips from Sand Hill Preservation Center at sandhillpreservation.com. I suggest you order in January or February, because the most in-demand varieties sell out extremely fast. If there is a company offering a larger selection than Sand Hill, I don't know about it. If you have a short growing season, choose varieties that mature in ninety days or less. You can visit Sand Hill's sweet potato catalog at: http://www.sandhillpreservation.com/pages/sweetpotato_catalog.html.

CREATING HOMEGROWN SWEET POTATO SLIPS

To grow slips, you need sweet potatoes that you have saved from your garden. You can purchase sweet potatoes, or even use some from the grocery store, but the ones at the store may be hybrid and have often been treated with chemicals or low-level radiation to discourage sprouting. The best way to get sweet potatoes is to order slips from a reputable grower like Sand Hill Preservation Center, grow them out, and save some sweet potatoes for growing your own slips the next year. Here are the steps for growing out slips for "sweets" (as sweet potatoes are called) in your backyard garden.

Step 1

In the second week of May, cover a section of your best garden soil with a cold frame or low growing tunnel for a week. For information on building

inexpensive cold frames that last decades, see my *Backyard Winter Gardening* book. The cold frame begins heating up the soil, using the warmth of the sun.

Step 2

In the third week of May, remove the cover temporarily. In the bed, dig a depression deep and long enough to fit your sweet potatoes and cover them with one inch of growing material—about three inches deep and six to eight inches wide.

Step 3

Line this depression with your sweet potatoes. Cover them with moist coconut coir or peat moss, pressed firmly around them. (They don't love soil. They prefer soilless mixes or extremely friable soil. They will not perform in clay soils). Water the area generously. Put the cold frame or low tunnel back in place.

Step 4

The sweet potatoes must remain continuously damp, hot, and humid three to five weeks. Water the sweet potatoes every day, preferably with warm water. They must never go dry, or the developing slips will be killed. If you have sunny weather, your first leafy slips will appear above the soil in about three weeks. If the weather has been cloudy and cool, it can take an extra week or two.

Step 5

Meanwhile, as you wait for the slips to grow, choose the place in your garden where you would like to plant the slips. To warm this soil in preparation for the slips, cover this empty section of your garden with a cold frame or low tunnel. This will allow the soil to begin naturally warming with the sun. Water the soil twice, once when you place the frame or tunnel over it, and a second time two weeks later.

Step 6

Your slips will be ready to transplant in June. When your slips have developed one or more leaves, carefully remove the soil around the slip and "slip" it off the sweet potato root by pinching or gently pulling. Don't move the sweet potato, because you can grow more slips, as will be explained in a moment. Ideally, one slip should have between one and three roots on it (just like onion threads). The more roots it has, the greater the transplant shock will be when the slips are moved to their permanent location, so it is best to use young, immature slips. Plant your slips in your prepared location so that just the roots are buried.

Don't confuse the methods used for planting potatoes with the methods used for planting sweet potatoes—they are totally different. Potatoes are planted deep. Sweet potatoes are planted shallowly. Sweet potatoes want a light soil that has good organic matter but not too much: don't plant them in pure compost, for example.

A mixture of compost, coir or peat moss, and clean (non-salty) sand is ideal. Water generously, preferably with warm water. Keep the cold frame or low tunnel in place for one to two weeks to allow your slips to become established, but be careful not to "cook" the slips with heat—there must be airflow, especially on sunny June days. If you are concerned that the weather is too hot and the slips might suffer, remove the covers during the day and replace them each night. Leave the covers on if the weather is cool. Remove the cover permanently once the weather is consistently hot. You can also plant your slips without the cover of a cold frame or low tunnel, but the small plants will likely just sit in the garden sluggishly until the truly hot weather warms up the soil.

Step 7

Now that you have carefully harvested and transplanted your slips, you can grow a second crop of slips from the same roots. Leave them in the cold frame or low tunnel. Make sure to re-bury them in any areas where you removed soil to harvest slips. Water generously, cover with the frame or tunnel, and keep moist and warm for one to three weeks until your second harvest of slips has appeared. These slips are generally ready to plant in July. You might be thinking that July is so late in the growing season that you won't get any harvest, but you are most likely wrong (keeping mind that you should use the short season varieties of sweet potatoes unless you live in an area with a long growing season). These July-harvested slips can be planted directly in the garden using the directions above, omitting the cold frame or low tunnel. Now that the July heat is present, the slips will grow exceedingly fast in your warm garden. Just make sure they have plenty of water. Remember that if you have a short growing season, you should be using sweet potato varieties that mature in ninety days or less. Sand Hill Preservation Center has many

such varieties, but they sell out quickly, so place your order early. Your slip order will not ship until late May or early June.

Note: The ideal size for harvesting sweet potatoes is smaller than you think, and certainly smaller than the sweet potatoes sold in many grocery stores. Remember that grocery store sweet potatoes, like common potatoes, are usually kept in a special chilled carbon dioxide storage chamber, without access to oxygen, which preserves them until they are ready to ship. Once they are ready to ship, they may be sprayed with chlorpropham, a chemical that Cornell University's toxicology report says is "moderately toxic by ingestion." The same report continued, "Symptoms of poisoning in laboratory animals have included listlessness, incoordination, nose bleeds, protruding eyes, bloody tears, difficulty in breathing, prostration, inability to urinate, high fevers, and death. Autopsies of animals have shown inflammation of the stomach and intestinal lining, congestion of the brain, lungs and other organs, and degenerative changes in the kidneys and liver."[1] They may also be legally exposed to low levels of radiation to inhibit sprouting in the warm, bright environment of the store. In the backyard garden, our goal is not to grow the largest sweet potatoes. Our goal is to grow the best sweet potatoes for flavor and winter storage. Here is advice from the Sand Hill Preservation Center website: "For many a sweet potato, the size of a nice fat bratwurst is about the best size for keeping and for baking. Bigger than that is ok, but they do not sprout as well nor keep as well because they suffer from bruising much easier." For information about sweet potatoes, growing, varieties, and more, visit sandhillpreservation.com. Those folks are not associated with this book, but I love their passion, their huge selection, and their expertise gained from years of growing experience.

Note: The biggest problem I have had growing "sweets" in my ninety-two-day growing season was not with getting usable roots (I do) but with getting to the roots before the voles. Voles are often mistaken for mice. Voles love my garden because, well, I'm lovable, I guess. They live in shallow tunnels under any rocks or wood they can find. As long as food is plentiful, they are not usually too much of a problem, but at the first sign of cold—just about the time when the sweet potatoes are ready to harvest—they start voraciously eating everything they can find. I have to keep a close eye on them, and I have learned the hard way that voles love sweet potatoes, so I should not delay in harvesting them. It is better to harvest smaller roots than no roots at all!

HOW TO PRESERVE

Sweet potatoes bruise easily and must be treated with care. Remember that unlike many common potatoes, sweet potatoes grow shallowly. Dig them up gently and carefully using your gloved hands and a garden fork. Do not wash them! Sweet potatoes, like all garden root vegetables, should not be washed for storage. Leave your sweet potatoes outside for a week in a place out of direct sunlight and not exposed to rain. This lets them "harden" and "cure" for storage. After a week, store them in a burlap or mesh bag like potatoes. Set them in the bag gently—sweet potatoes bruise even more easily than common potatoes. Sweet potatoes with any damage should be used first and not stored with the others, because a rotting sweet potato can spoil the others around it. Store in low humidity in a cool, dry, dark place.

Note: Ants tunnel into both potatoes and sweet potatoes, and these roots with holes in them will quickly rot while left outside to cure. Instead of curing them, eat them immediately after harvest. Tubers with holes should not be used for storage, as they will rot.

RECOMMENDED VARIETIES

In the Sand Hill catalog, you will find different colors: white, purple, orange, yellow, pink, and red. Some produce huge vines more than a dozen feet long. Some grow just on a small bush. Choose the varieties that suit your space and curiosity.

HOW TO SAVE SLIPS

Save your last sweet potato roots for growing slips the next year in the process described above.

Are all slips heirloom? No. Slips from hybrid parents will be unstable, meaning they will have unpredictable traits.

NOTES

1.   "Clorpropham," Extension Toxicology Network, accessed October 19, 2016, http://pmep. cce.cornell.edu/profiles/extoxnet/carbaryl-dicrotophos/chlorpropham-ext.html.

SWISS CHARD

SEED-CLEANING METHOD
Thresh and winnow

RECOMMENDED VARIETIES
Bright lights swiss chard (also called rainbow mix) has yellow, red, purple and green stems and tastes good too. Bright lights can change color depending on temperature and is most often red when grown in winter in my geothermal greenhouse. Bright lights easily self-seeds in a no-till garden, and if you plant it once and allow some plants to go to seed, you will likely have swiss chard growing in your garden for the rest of your life.

HOW TO SAVE SEEDS
Swiss chard bolts to seed in the second year. A few plants may try to bolt to seed in the first year, especially if exposed to drought conditions. These should not be allowed to go to seed, because you don't want to encourage plants that go straight to seed instead of being harvestable for a year before

Swiss chard seeds

SPECIES:	*Beta vulgaris*
EASY TO SAVE SEEDS?	Likely yes, if planting one variety per year within one species.
SEED TYPE REQUIRED FOR SEED SAVING:	Heirloom (open-pollinated) seeds (available at SeedRenaissance.com).
NUMBER OF VARIETIES AVAILABLE:	Several
LIFE SPAN OF PLANT:	Biennial
LIFE SPAN OF SEED:	Germination decreases after six years of ideal storage. Ideal storage means avoiding drastic temperature fluctuations by keeping seeds in a cool, dark, dry place.
SEED MATURATION:	Allow seeds to dry fully on the plant in the garden or mature as long as possible in garden, pull up the whole plant, roots and all, and dry in a cool dark place, like a garage. Then harvest seeds.
FLOWER TYPE:	Perfect
SEX TYPE:	Outbreeding
CROSSES WITH:	All varieties of chard, beets, sugar beets, and mangels.
POLLINATION TYPE:	Wind
SEEDS IN WHAT YEAR?	Second year
ISOLATION DISTANCE:	Two miles
SHATTERING RATE:	Slow
POPULATION MINIMUM:	10+ plants

going to seed. Swiss chard usually easily overwinters even in cold zones and hard winters, but if you live in zone 4 or lower, you may want to cover your swiss chard in winter with a cold frame, cloche, row cover, or other protection.

Up to a third of the leaves may be harvested from plants being kept for seeds, but only in the first year. In the second year, the leaves should not be harvested, so that the plant can have enough energy to seed successfully.

In the second year, the plants will begin to bolt to seed as soon as the weather warms. A group of ten or more plants of the same variety should be allowed to go to flower for best quality seed. Too few plants will mean low seed germination, few seeds, or genetic bottlenecks in the seed that will appear as inbreeding in future generations of the seed. This inbreeding will appear most prominently as color loss among your variety—if you do not have enough colors in seed, the plants will slowly all drift toward red through the next

generations. For the best color outcome, you may want to allow ten plants of each color to go to seed. The color mix has been fairly stable in my garden through many years now, and I just allow all my plants to go to seed (on years when I am not saving beet seeds). The color of swiss chard is also affected by temperature.

Swiss chard seed generally dries on the stem before the stem fully dries. The seed will scatter naturally if left too long on the stem once it's dry. Harvest it by stripping the seed from the stem with your hand while wearing leather gloves. Put a large bowl under the plant or cover the ground with a cloth to capture the seeds. Remember that swiss chard will cross with other chard varieties, beets, sugar beets, and mangels. Only one variety of Beta vulgaris should be allowed to flower in a year. For example, if you allow any variety of beet to flower at the same time as any variety of swiss chard, the plants will cross-pollinate and the resulting seeds will not produce true offspring.

After you have harvested the swiss chard seeds, spread them in a single layer on cookie sheets and leave them outside for several hours to let any insects depart. Then allow them to air-dry indoors for several days. Once fully dry, store in a cool, dry, dark place until you are ready to use them.

TOMATOES

SEED-CLEANING METHOD

Cut an "x" into the bottom of the tomato. Squeeze seeds into a bowl. Wash and air-dry indoors on a nonstick surface, such as a silicone baking tray liner or wax paper. Seeds should never be dried in a machine or oven. Alternatively, you may add a half-cup of water to the seeds you have collected in the bowl and allow them to sit in a sunny spot for several days until the bowl is covered with white mold. This process breaks down the gelatin sac surrounding each seed. Remove and discard the mold. Wash seeds and air-dry indoors on a nonstick surface as described above.

Second alternative

You can squeeze seeds from the tomato onto a paper towel and allow them to completely dry. The seeds will not come off the paper towel, but you can cut or rip up the paper towel as needed the next year when planting seeds.

Washed tomato seeds

RECOMMENDED VARIETIES

I have probably tested six hundred varieties of heirloom tomatoes, and I test about fifty more each year. Out of all of these, here are the varieties I recommend:

Stupice

This is an old Siberian variety that is always the earliest produce tomatoes in my garden. These are determinate, meaning they set fruit in a short period of time, which makes them great for canning or freezing. Seeds are available at SeedRenaissance.com.

German Queen

A visitor who came to tour my garden handed me the first German Queen I had ever seen, and wow, what a tomato it is! These ripen just before the first frost in my garden, but they are huge. Every single tomato is over a pound, and some are over two pounds! They are great slicers, and we use them extensively for making and freezing sauce. Seeds available at SeedRenaissance.com.

Roma

This is an old favorite, developed in Italy and used as a favorite saucing tomato for centuries. Why? Because this variety is low on seeds and juice and heavy on thick, delicious flesh that makes a wonderful, rich tomato sauce. Seeds available at SeedRenaissance.com.

Amish Paste

Like Roma, these are huge, fleshy saucing tomatoes that are also low on seeds and juice with thick flesh and perfect flavor for sauce or sandwiches. Seeds available at SeedRenaissance.com.

Snow Fairy

This Siberian variety is the best for greenhouse and winter production of tomatoes. Probably no one in the world has tested as many winter tomato varieties as I have, and this one is hands down the winner! Seeds available at SeedRenaissance.com.

HOW TO SAVE SEEDS

There are two methods, which both work equally well.

Method 1

When the tomato is ripe or overly ripe, cut off the bottom and squeeze the tomato over a bowl to capture the juice, gel, and seeds. Wash away the juice and gel by spraying warm water over the seeds in a fine-mesh sieve (fine enough that the seeds won't slip through the mesh). Spread the washed seeds on a clean white paper towel and allow them to dry completely over several days. Write the variety name on the paper towel. When the seed are completely dry, fold up the paper towel and store in a dry place until you are ready to plant the seeds the next year. The seeds will be stuck to the paper towel. Simply cut up the paper towel around the seeds and plant each seed with the paper towel on it. Washed seeds can also be dried on a silicone baking liner and scraped off with a rubber spatula for storage.

Tomato seeds in a sieve

Method 2

When the tomato is ripe or overly ripe, cut off the bottom and squeeze the tomato over a bowl to capture the juice, gel, and seeds. Squeeze in as many tomatoes of the same variety as you wish.

SPECIES:	*Solanum lycopersicum* (syn. *Lycopersicon esculentum*)
EASY TO SAVE SEEDS?	Likely yes, if planting one variety per year within one species. However, some species (often called potato leaf tomato varieties) produce a stamen that extrudes from the flower and can allow insects to cross-pollinate among such plants. Tomato varieties that do not have an extruding stamen are self-pollinating, and no isolation is needed. Tomato varieties that have an extruding stamen may need isolation up to a mile. Stamen-extruding varieties do not cross with non-stamen-extruding varieties.
SEED TYPE REQUIRED FOR SEED SAVING:	Heirloom (open-pollinated) seeds (available at SeedRenaissance.com).
NUMBER OF VARIETIES AVAILABLE:	Many
LIFE SPAN OF PLANT:	Annual in most of the United States.
LIFE SPAN OF SEED:	Germination decreases after four to ten years of ideal storage, depending on the variety. Ideal storage means avoiding drastic temperature fluctuations by keeping seeds in a cool, dark, dry place.
SEED MATURATION:	Seeds are ready to harvest when the tomato is ripe.
FLOWER TYPE:	Perfect
SEX TYPE:	Most types are inbreeding
POLLINATION TYPE:	Self-pollinating and limited insect-pollinating.
SEEDS IN WHAT YEAR?	First year
SHATTERING RATE:	Not applicable
POPULATION MINIMUM:	3+ plants

Set the bowl outside or out of the way for several days (may take up to a week) indoors or outdoors, away from direct sunlight and safe from animals. Over these days, a white mold will form on the top of the bowl and the seeds will sink to the bottom of the bowl. The gel sacs around the seeds will open, releasing the seeds. The mold helps to kill some varieties of seed-borne disease. After three days, skim off and discard the mold. Wash away the juice and gel by spraying hot water over the seeds in a fine-mesh sieve (fine enough that the seeds won't slip through the mesh.) Spread the washed seeds in a single layer (as much as possible) on a silicone baking liner or wax paper. Allow to air dry for several days until fully dry. Scrape off the seeds with a rubber spatula and store in a cool, dark, dry place in a container until ready to use.

Washed tomato seeds on silicone liner

TURNIPS

SEED-CLEANING METHOD

Thresh and winnow. When the seedpods are dry, rub them to release the seeds, or uproot the plant carefully and hit it against the inside of a large box or plastic storage container to release and capture the seeds. Be careful when touching the dried plant in the garden, because the slightest shaking can cause hundreds of seeds to fall to the ground. You may want to place an old sheet on the ground under the plant before trying to harvest seeds or uproot the plant.

RECOMMENDED VARIETIES

Golden Ball Turnips
These do not look or taste like traditional turnips. They have a pale yellow flesh with a mildly sweet flavor. They are a favorite at our house.

Purple Top White Globe Turnip
Purple top white globes have a wonderful heirloom turnip taste and are a very hardy plant, great for using in roast vegetable dishes and soups. They have a beautiful purple top around a white globe with white flesh inside. Purple top white globe is an excellent self-seeder as long as you keep it isolated from other *Brassica rapa* varieties. It's an old, standard variety that does great in winter greenhouses! Seeds available at SeedRenaissance.com.

HOW TO SAVE SEEDS

Turnip seeds are harvested from second-year bulbs. Learning to harvest turnip seeds begins with a caution: some turnips might try to bolt (produce seed stalks) in the first year, especially if they are exposed to drought conditions. Don't allow seed to form from first-year bulbs, and do not harvest seed from first-year bulbs. Why? Turnips over the centuries have been "trained" by gardeners to form a bulb for harvesting. Their natural inclination is to form seeds instead of a bulb. If you harvest seed from first-year plants, within a few generations of seed, you will have turnips that produce only seeds and not root bulbs for eating. The roots will be skinny and useless—and then you have defeated the purpose of having the seed. To correctly produce turnip seed, follow these steps:

Step 1:
Plant turnip seeds and allow them to mature through the summer.

Step 2:
Carefully harvest the mature turnips and select the best and most perfect specimens for seed-saving. Caution: only allow one variety of turnip to flower in your garden. If two or more varieties flower at the same time, they will cross, which means your seed will be unstable. Unstable seed may produce seed like either parent or a combination of the two. Unstable seed may not continue to produce good bulbs after several generations, and you will not be able to predict the traits, including color, flavor, or size, of the turnips produced. For these reasons, be sure that you save turnip bulbs from only one heirloom variety per year. The good news is that with ten seed plants, you will produce more than enough turnip seed for several years of gardening, so you will be able to select a new variety for seed saving the next year.

Step 3:
Cut the leaves off the turnips you have selected for seed saving. You may leave up to an inch of stem. Caution: do not cut the bulb of the turnip itself. Even a small cut or scar may cause the turnip to spoil in storage. Do not trim or damage the roots. Store these bulbs through winter in damp sand, sawdust, or pine shavings in a cool, dry, dark place such as a garage, basement cold room, or cellar. The temperature in your storage space must be cool, but it cannot go below freezing or the turnips will likely freeze and spoil. Some "experts" will argue that each different vegetable should be stored at a precise temperature and humidity, requiring expensive equipment. This violates the law of abundance in the garden. Turnips have been saved in cellars—without precise scientific measurements—for centuries. They are easy to store and do not require "precise" temperatures or humidity. Some may rot in storage. This is natural and they should be discarded.

SPECIES:	*Brassica rapa*
EASY TO SAVE SEEDS?	Likely yes, if planting one variety per year within one species. Note: Birds may compete with you for the seeds.
SEED TYPE REQUIRED FOR SEED SAVING:	Heirloom (open-pollinated) seeds (available at SeedRenaissance.com).
NUMBER OF VARIETIES AVAILABLE:	Several
LIFE SPAN OF PLANT:	Biennial
LIFE SPAN OF SEED:	Germination decreases after five years of ideal storage. Ideal storage means avoiding drastic temperature fluctuations by keeping seeds in a cool, dark, dry place.
SEED MATURATION:	Allow seeds to dry fully on the plant in the garden or mature as long as possible in garden, pull up the whole plant, roots and all, and dry in a cool dark place, like a garage. Then harvest seeds.
FLOWER TYPE:	Perfect
SEX TYPE:	Outbreeding
CROSSES WITH:	All varieties of turnip, as well as all varieties of Chinese cabbage, broccoli raab, and Chinese mustards, including mizuna.
POLLINATION TYPE:	Insect
SEEDS IN WHAT YEAR?	Second year (some varieties may be first year)
ISOLATION DISTANCE:	One mile
SHATTERING RATE:	Quick
POPULATION MINIMUM:	10+ plants

The turnips will slowly produce leaves in the dark. Pick these leaves off monthly, as they take energy away from the bulb. The leaves are edible and great in salads or green smoothies. *Caution:* if you are also preserving turnips for eating, make sure you don't mix up the turnips you are keeping for eating with the turnips you are keeping for seed, or you might eat your future seed-producing bulbs. This might seem like a unimportant concern, but if you are in the middle of making soup or roasted vegetables in December and you ask a child or spouse to "grab" some turnips out of storage for you and they bring the bulbs you have selected for seed-saving without you realizing it, you have lost your potential for a seed crop.

Step 4:

In the spring of the second year, plant the saved root bulbs in the outside garden as soon as the soil can be worked. If you are concerned that the soil may refreeze in the garden, wait to plant the bulbs (keeping in mind that the longer you wait, the more likely the turnips are to rot, costing you your seed crop), or cover the planted bulbs with a cold frame. (For information on cold frames, see my *Backyard Winter Gardening* book.) The bulbs will bolt (begin to form seed stalks) in early summer. The seeds are mature when the plants begin to dry up and die. Caution: turnip seeds are excellent at planting themselves. When dry, turnip seeds are scattered by wind, rain, and birds. Once they are scattered, they are difficult to retrieve and may spoil if you try to save them because they are damp or muddy. Luckily, turnip seeds tend to dry before the stems that hold them. To prevent scattering, harvest the seeds after they turn white but before the stem fades from green to white (or red) and dies. To harvest the seed, lay a cloth or tarp on the ground under the plant. Wearing a leather glove, put your hand at the base of each turnip stem and pull upward, knocking the seeds off the stem onto the tarp. Turnip seeds are fairly large and woody. They are generally white in color and can be as large as the size of a pea or a bit smaller.

Turnip flower

Step 5:

Once you have harvested the seeds, allow them to air-dry outside for several hours, up to a full day. This allows any bugs time to leave the seeds before you bring them indoors. However, while you are airing your seeds outdoors, make sure they will not be exposed to water, wind, or birds.

Step 6:

Bring the seeds indoors for several days to dry. Air-drying should be done indoors to avoid weather, moisture, wind, and birds. Once seeds are completely dry, they can be stored in a paper, glass, or plastic container.

WATERMELON

SEED-CLEANING METHOD

Remove seeds from the melon. Wash and air-dry indoors before storage. Seeds should never be dried in a machine or oven.

RECOMMENDED VARIETIES

Any heirloom variety with a day count that fits in your growing season.

White Sugar Lump

This is an exceedingly rare watermelon variety. This variety is hugely important because it is far and away the best variety I have ever found for growing without plastic. It is prolific with no plastic. Unfortunately, I am not joking when I say the seeds are almost extinct. Where I live, it is impossible to grow out "true" watermelon seed that is not cross-pollinated by neighbors' watermelon plants, so I have not yet been able to save this variety, but I do have some seeds. I have found a reliable volunteer with a huge, remote property who has agreed to grow out a crop of these seeds for me, so I hope that for the time being, I can at least offer these seeds for sale again. Watermelons are not easy to hand-pollinate and keep pure, so for the moment, I am still working on saving these seeds the old-fashioned way—by growing them in isolation. This old variety (1) tastes great, (2) ripens early, and (3) grows well without black plastic. This is a so-called "icebox" melon, meaning that when it is mature, it is about the size of your head. This is also a great melon because the flesh inside is entirely white—but tastes just like red watermelon. Check SeedRenaissance.com for availability.

HOW TO SAVE SEEDS

Watermelon seeds are harvested from overly ripe watermelons. Watermelon seeds that are harvested from melons that are just ripe and not overly ripe may not be fully developed, and may not be viable. Not every seed inside a watermelon matures on the same day or at the same time, so it is very possible that if you harvest seeds from a melon that is just "ripe" then you may have some seeds that are viable (will germinate when planted) and some that aren't. Science refers to this as the seed germination rate. For the best germination rate—meaning the highest number of usable seeds— watermelon seed should be harvested from watermelons just as the melon begins to soften and spoil.

To correctly produce watermelon seed, plant watermelon seeds and allow them to mature through the summer. In autumn, select only the best and most perfect specimens for seed saving. Caution: only allow one variety of watermelon to flower in your garden. If two or more varieties flower at the same time, they will cross, which means your seed will be unstable—unpredictable in size,

SPECIES:	*Citrullus lanatus*
EASY TO SAVE SEEDS?	Likely yes, if planting one variety per year within one species.
SEED TYPE REQUIRED FOR SEED SAVING:	Heirloom (open-pollinated) seeds (available at SeedRenaissance.com).
NUMBER OF VARIETIES AVAILABLE:	Several
LIFE SPAN OF PLANT:	Annual
LIFE SPAN OF SEED:	Germination decreases after six years of ideal storage. Ideal storage means avoiding drastic temperature fluctuations by keeping seeds in a cool, dark, dry place.
SEED MATURATION:	Store the ripe watermelon until it begins to soften, or for forty-five days, whichever comes first. Then remove the seeds. Wash and dry before storage. Seeds from watermelons that are not stored until soft may have a low germination rate.
FLOWER TYPE:	Monoecious
SEX TYPE:	Outbreeding
CROSSES WITH:	All varieties of watermelon and citron. Does not cross with cantaloupe, honeydew, casaba, or other members of the cantaloupe species.
POLLINATION TYPE:	Insect
SEEDS IN WHAT YEAR?	First year
ISOLATION DISTANCE:	One-half mile
SHATTERING RATE:	None
POPULATION MINIMUM:	10+ plants

shape, color, and flavor—and won't look like the melons produced by the parent plants. These "wild" traits will become more pronounced with each generation of new seed.

A real problem for backyard gardeners who want to save watermelon seeds is raccoons and other creatures who delight in eating the center of the fruits just as they ripen. However, for highest germination, the watermelons that you want to save seed from should be left in the garden, or in storage in a cold, dark, dry place, as long as possible so the melons can over-ripen and go soft as they begin to rot. This is the ideal time to harvest the watermelon seed. Raccoons and other creatures are famous for coming into the garden at night and eating the entire center out of the melons—sometimes seeds and all. The longer you leave a ripe melon in the garden, the more you are tempting fate because creatures will be drawn to the smell. To be safe, you may want to harvest half or more of your melons as they ripen, eat them, and save the seeds with the understanding that you may have a lower seed germination rate. Then you can leave some melons to go soft in the garden and begin to rot, and harvest seeds from those plants. To keep those plants safe until you harvest them, it may be a good idea to wrap them completely in a ball of chicken wire. Watermelon varieties that are specifically grown for "keeping" should not be cracked open until they just begin to go soft, so the seeds have as much time to mature inside the melon as possible.

Separate the seeds from the watermelon flesh either by picking out the seeds, by mashing the flesh and squeezing out the seeds in your hands, or by mashing the flesh by rubbing it between your hands to fully separate it. The flesh can be discarded. Rinse the seeds in cool water and dry them for several days in a single layer on wax paper, parchment, or a silicone baking liner. Once the seeds are fully dry, they can be stored at room temperature in a dry place.

WHERE DO SEEDLESS WATERMELONS COME FROM?

"The obvious question asked about growing seedless watermelons is, 'How does one obtain seed of a seedless watermelon?' Obviously, you cannot save seed from a seedless watermelon. So, where do the seeds come from? Simply stated, the number of chromosomes (the threadlike bodies within cells that contain the inheritance units called genes) in a normal watermelon plant is doubled by the use of the chemical colchicine. Doubling a normal (diploid) watermelon results in a tetraploid plant (one having four sets of chromosomes). When the tetraploid plant is bred back, or pollinated, by a diploid or normal plant, the resulting seed produces a triploid plant that is basically a "mule" of the plant kingdom, and it produces seedless watermelons. Seeds of seedless varieties are available from most major seed companies."

Jerry Parsons, Larry Stein, Tom Longbrake, Sam Cotner, and Jerral Johnson, "Where Do Seedless Watermelons Come From?" *Lawn and Garden Update*, May–June 2000, http://aggie-horticulture.tamu.edu/newsletters/hortupdate/hortupdate_archives/2000/may00/h5may00.html.

ABOUT THE AUTHOR

CALEB WARNOCK is the owner of SeedRenaissance.com, where he sells only heirloom seed varieties that he has evaluated in an organic garden for performance in earliness, flavor, production, storage, cold-soil tolerance, winter harvest ability, and self-seeding capacity, without petrochemical fertilizer, pesticides, or herbicides. If he doesn't love a variety, he doesn't sell it. Every seed is guaranteed pure—*never* hybrid, GMO, patented, or corporate owned. "Our food supply *must* remain in the public domain," Caleb says. "Join me in creating a renaissance in our backyard gardens."

Caleb was raised in the kitchens and gardens of the last generation to provide family meals without relying on the grocery store. He has won more than a dozen awards for journalism and literature, and he regularly teaches "forgotten skills" classes on topics ranging from winter greenhouse construction, cheese making, cold frame gardening, and more. To reach the author, visit CalebWarnock.blogspot.com or email calebwarnock@yahoo.com.

SCAN TO VISIT

CALEBWARNOCK.BLOGSPOT.COM